The
WORD OF WISDOM
FOOD PLAN

—A—
MEDICAL
REVIEW
OF THE
MORMON
DOCTRINE

The
WORD OF WISDOM
FOOD PLAN

—A—
MEDICAL
REVIEW
OF THE
MORMON
DOCTRINE

By
Kenneth E. Johnson, M.D.

For information contact:
  KEJ PenMed
  2166 CR 500
  Bayfield, CO 81122

ISBN: 1-55517-118-4
Library of Congress Catalog Card Number: 93-71489

Published and distributed by:

CFI
Cedar Fort, Incorporated
925 North Main, Springville, UT 84663 801-489-4084

Cover Design by Lyle Mortimer
Typeset by Brian Carter
Lithographed in the United States of America

TABLE OF CONTENTS

ACKNOWLEDGEMENTS

I would like to thank Marilyn Nelson who finally connected me to a computer;

Elizabeth Mixon for reviewing my first drafts and making valuable suggestions;

Kathy Frandson for her editorial expertise;

Joan Paine, a librarian, for finding the references to document the medical facts; and

Frances Smeath for converting a medical clinician into a writer.

Special accolades should be given to Joann, my wife, who joins me this year in a 50th wedding anniversary celebration. We met in grade school, dated in high school, and married when I was in medical school. She has been a great mother and wife—for too much of the time I have been immersed in medical and church activities. I salute and pay honor to her for the years that she has had to put up with me.

Thanks are expressed to Lyle Mortimer, Brian Carter and the others at CFI for their publishing skills.

FOREWORD

Every aspect of modern life seems to have changed dramatically in just a few years. Nowhere is this more apparent than in the foods we eat. Microwaves and fast-food restaurants were all but unheard of a generation ago, but are now everywhere, along with an ever-growing array of appliances that modernize our kitchens. The emphasis is on convenience and speed of preparation.

At the same time, modern medical science has made discoveries about the power of foods that prevent illness and improve our sense of well-being. With knowledge about saturated fat, fiber, complex carbohydrates, and cholesterol, we are discovering, ironically enough, that the foods with the greatest power to protect the health of the body are the humble foods that have been familiar since long before the appearance of electric appliances or analytical scientists. The vegetables, fruits, grains, and beans that grow in the earth and are prepared in the simplest of ways bring us powerful nutrients that keep our bodies strong and our senses sharp, while animal products have been proven to be unnecessary and often harmful.

Understanding this new wisdom and putting it to use is the purpose of this book. As you turn its pages, you will find both scientific facts and practical information that can revolutionize your health and that of your loved ones.

Neal D. Barnard, M.D., President
Physicians Committee for Responsible Medicine

INTRODUCTION

THE WORD OF WISDOM FOOD PLAN

A DISEASE PREVENTION DIET

IN MATTERS OF HEALTH TODAY WE LARGELY CONTROL
OUR OWN WELL BEING.

A few generations ago, uncontrollable infections were the major cause of illness and death. These acute diseases are now largely prevented by modern medical science, with the development and help of antibiotics, vaccinations, water sanitation, proper waste disposal, food laws, mosquito control and earlier, better medical care.

With the control of these acute infectious diseases, we now have a new set of diseases that make us sick and cause premature death. They are heart disease, stroke, cancer, diabetes, high blood pressure, obesity and osteoporosis.

We all want good health. But these diseases are rampant among us. What must we do to promote better health and prevent early death from these diseases? Reputable experts have some good answers to offer, and the good news is that each one of us can largely prevent the development of these diseases by the choices we make.

Dr. James O. Mason, one of the authors of "Encyclopedia of Mormonism" and former Assistant Secretary of the U.S. Department of Health said, "Today more than two thirds of premature deaths are due mostly to chronic illness and conditions which are aided and abetted by people's own lifestyle choices."[1]

---

[1] *Deseret News*, "Church News" Section, (December, 1992), p. 6.

In 1988, Dr. C. Everett Koop, then U.S. Surgeon General, further focused on lifestyle choices when he said that 68% of all deaths in the United States are diet related.[1] These facts are validated by the 1989 report, "Diet and Health," published by the National Research Council.[2] Both reports document the relationship between diet and the high incidence of cancer, heart disease and strokes.

Today, members of the LDS church have the benefit of sound medical knowledge and the blessing of revealed truth to guide their lifestyle choices, especially their food choices. They, in a real sense, choose whether or not they have good health.

In this book I will present anew the counsel of LDS church leaders beginning with Joseph Smith's 160-year-old revelation, the Word of Wisdom. I will also present the medical and scientific facts known today that confirm its truth.

This book is written to encourage you and your family to improve your lifestyles. You do have a choice. By following all the tenets of the Word of Wisdom, a longer and healthier life with great temporal and spiritual blessings is assured. In addition you will look better, feel better, save money and lose excess weight.

When the Word of Wisdom was revealed to Joseph Smith in 1833, people knew virtually nothing about the harm of tobacco, the degradation of alcohol addiction, nor the effect of caffeine on the body. The Saints, who obeyed this law of health as best they could, did so by faith, not by knowledge. By inspiration, the church leaders gave direction to the Saints. There was gradual compliance by the faithful concerning tea, coffee, tobacco and alcohol. Mormons are now well known and admired for their stand on these health issues.

The focus in this book, however, is not about the narrow and well-understood connection between Mormons and abstinence from these harmful substances. The Word of Wisdom revelation is much more than that.

---

[1] *The Surgeon General's Report on Nutrition and Health,* United States Department of Health and Human Services, (Rocklin, CA: Prima Publishing and Communications, 1988).

[2] "Diet and Health: Implications for Reducing Chronic Disease Risk," National Research Council, (Washington, DC: National Academy Press, 1989).

It is a "law of total health." Dr. Alvin K. Benson, BYU professor of geophysics and geology, used that term to describe the Word of Wisdom in a Joseph Smith symposium. He also said,

> It's exciting to see how continuing scientific discoveries verify the wisdom and insight revealed to the Prophet in the Word of Wisdom, a revelation given when knowledge of nutrition was essentially nonexistent.[1]

The bright light of recent scientific and medical advances is focusing new attention on the nutritional aspects of the Word of Wisdom. I call these the Word of Wisdom food plan because they give specific instructions about our food choices.

The full text of this remarkable revelation follows now, to provide easy access for members of the LDS Church and a reference for nonmembers. The food portion is italicized for emphasis. No other changes have been made.

Section 89 of Doctrine and Covenants. Revelation given through Joseph Smith the Prophet, at Kirtland, Ohio, February 27, 1833, known today as the Word of Wisdom.

1. A Word of Wisdom, for the benefit of the council of high priests, assembled in Kirtland, and the church, and also the saints in Zion—
2. To be sent greeting; not by commandment or constraint, but by revelation and the word of wisdom, showing forth the order and will of God in the temporal salvation of all saints in the last days—
3. Given for a principle with promise, adapted to the capacity of the weak and the weakest of all saints, who are or can be called saints.
4. Behold, verily, thus saith the Lord unto you: In consequence of evils and designs which do and will exist in the hearts of conspiring men in the last days, I have warned you, and forewarn you, by giving unto you this word of wisdom by revelation—
5. That inasmuch as any man drinketh wine or strong drink among you, behold it is not good, neither meet in the sight of your Father, only in assembling yourselves together to offer up your sacraments before him.
6. And, behold, this should be wine, yea, pure wine of the grape of the vine, of your own make.
7. And, again, strong drinks are not for the belly, but for the washing of your bodies.

---

[1] *Deseret News*, "Church News" Section, (February, 1992).

8. And again, tobacco is not for the body, neither for the belly, and is not good for man, but is an herb for bruises and all sick cattle, to be used with judgment and skill.
9. And again, hot drinks are not for the body or belly.
10. And again, verily I say unto you, *all wholesome herbs* God hath ordained for the constitution, nature, and use of man—
11. *Every herb in the season thereof,* and *every fruit in the season thereof;* all these to be used with prudence and thanksgiving.
12. Yea, *flesh also of beasts and of the fowls* of the air, I, the Lord, have ordained for the use of man with thanksgiving; nevertheless *they are to be used sparingly;*
13. And it is pleasing unto me that they should not be used, *only in times of winter, or of cold, or famine.*
14. *All grain is ordained for the use of man and of beasts, to be the staff of life,* not only for man but for the *beasts of the field,* and the *fowls* of heaven, and *all wild animals* that run or creep on the earth;
15. And *these* hath God made for the use of man *only in times of famine and excess of hunger.*
16. *All grain is good for the food of man;* as *also* the *fruit* of the vine; that which yieldeth fruit, whether in the ground or above the ground—
17. Nevertheless, wheat for man, and corn for the ox, and oats for the horse, and rye for the fowls and for swine, and for all beasts of the field, and barley for all useful animals, and for mild drinks, as also other grain.
18. And all saints who remember to keep and do these sayings, walking in obedience to the commandments, shall receive health in their navel and marrow to their bones;
19. And shall find wisdom and great treasures of knowledge, even hidden treasures;
20. And shall run and not be weary, and shall walk and not faint.
21. And I, the Lord, give unto them a promise, that the destroying angel shall pass by them, as the children of Israel, and not slay them. Amen. (*emphasis added*)

As one reads carefully the italicized portion of the Word of Wisdom, one must ponder what one is being told about eating the flesh of beasts and fowl. One should especially pay attention to the word "sparingly" in verse 12, and note that "sparingly" is defined in verse 13 and defined for the second time in verse 15. It must be important. Furthermore, "sparingly" does not mean "in moderation." The adverb means "severely restricted" and "only under certain circumstances" as it defines the eating of flesh of beasts and fowl in the revelation.

In addition to concern about the word "sparingly," there should be concern and a greater appreciation of the phrase "All grain is ordained...to be the staff of life" (D&C 89:14). This phrase, "staff of life," strongly suggests that our major food should be grains.

These two interpretations will be viewed in the light of discourses of past and present church leaders and in the light of recent medical knowledge.

But before documenting our present day knowledge, let us go back and review the health and medical conditions that existed at the time when the Word of Wisdom first came to light.

CHAPTER ONE

MEDICINE AND RELIGION IN 1833

When the Word of Wisdom was revealed in 1833 to the prophet Joseph Smith, he and the small band of church converts were living mostly in the Kirtland, Ohio area. Just a year earlier Joseph Smith had been dragged out of his home by a mob, beaten, choked unconscious, tarred, feathered, and nearly killed. The men tried to force poison down his mouth, breaking one of his teeth in the scuffle. This caused a lisp or slight whistle when he talked until the tooth was later repaired in Nauvoo, Illinois.

The state of Ohio was still a small-town frontier, with men and their families clearing land for farming; the new European immigrants were looking for a new life. The townspeople who settled Ohio were characterized by a sense of rugged individualism.

Great chaos reigned. As white settlers clamored for more land, Indians were moved off their land to a "permanent" home west of the Mississippi River, through ninety-four treaties shamefully passed by Congress and signed by President Andrew Jackson. Indians of many different tribes streamed through the frontier states as they were pushed west. Church immigrants began to arrive from Europe, and the ill-fated and temporary Missouri migration of the Saints was about to begin.

Religious fervor was strong among both members and nonmembers of the church. Diverse religious sects, church revivals, circuit preachers, and predictions of the imminent end of the world were common. The concept of Christ's Second Advent was an inter-church doctrine prominent among Baptist, First Christian, and Methodist ministers.

It was in this setting that a new church sect, the Seventh Day Adventists, began preparing for Christ's Second Advent, which they predicted would be on October 22, 1844. They based their prediction primarily on an interpretation of Daniel 8:13-19.

When compared to today's health standards, those of 1833 were despicable. Epidemics of infectious disease swept through entire communities; diphtheria, whooping cough, measles, mumps, tuberculosis, and typhoid were common. A person living to the age of forty would have survived years with one disease or another, and sickness was the norm.

Only the very wealthy could afford glass windows, so flies and mosquitoes infested the homes. Water from streams contaminated by animal wastes supplied most families, and few people had the luxury of bathing. People were often sewn into long winter underwear in the fall, and did not remove them until spring.

Tuberculosis was widespread, and carried with it draining sores, coughs, fevers, sweats, and weight loss. Joseph Smith's mother, Lucy, was ill with tuberculosis early in her life; both his aunts, Lovina and Lovisa, died of the disease. Lucy had a miraculous recovery from tuberculosis, and later bore several children, including the prophet.

Epidemic typhoid infected Joseph Smith in early childhood, and complications of the disease affected the bones of his shoulder and left leg. When Joseph refused to have the leg amputated, doctors used a new technique now called saucerization to clean out the infected area. Lacking the blessing of anesthetics, young Joseph screamed loudly as the doctors removed large pieces of infected bone. The leg gradually healed, but Joseph had to walk with crutches for a long time.

Another incident illustrates how primitive medical care was during the first half of the nineteenth century. Less than two months after Joseph Smith was visited by the Angel Moroni on September 21, 1823, Joseph's oldest brother, Alvin, became sick with "bilious colic" (which we now think was acute appendicitis). A Dr. Greenwood treated him by administering at least one heavy dose of calomel, a purgative now known to be a poison. Alvin worsened and died on November 19, 1823. During an autopsy, the calomel was found lodged in a gangrenous bowel. This same finding was seen so often that the Surgeon General banned the use of calomel forty years later during the Civil War.

DOMESTIC MEDICINE

Medical treatment during these times was often nonexistent or crude, if not actually harmful. Those on the western frontier had to solve their own problems: roads were bad, transportation was poor, and isolation required that families take care of themselves.

Women stored medicinal herbs and food for the winter, and a network of kin and community gave advice and assistance when illness struck. In particularly worrisome cases, families called in an older woman who had a reputation for skill with the sick.

In this setting appeared books written by purported medical experts to aid families in caring for themselves. Written in common language, the books avoided Latin or technical terms. The best-known was William Buchan's *Domestic Medicine*,[1] described in its subtitle as "an attempt to render the Medical Art more generally useful, by showing people what is in their own power both with respect to the Prevention and Cure of Diseases." Buchan stated that physicians were rarely needed and "that everything valuable in the practical part of medicine is within reach of common sense."

In 1830, the year the LDS Church was organized, John C. Gunn published another popular book, also titled *Domestic Medicine*.[2] Its title page declared that it was "arranged on a New Simple Plan, By Which the Practice of Medicine is Reduced to Principles of Common Sense" and was "Intended Expressly for Benefit of Families." Gunn proclaimed that "the more nearly we can place men on a level in point of knowledge, the happier we would become in society with each other, and the less danger there would be of tyranny."

Healing by faith was practiced in many Christian homes along the western frontier during the early 1800s, patterned after the well-known

---

[1] Buchan, W., *Domestic Medicine or the Family Physician*, (Philadelphia, 1771), For various editions of his work in America, see Francesco Guerra, *American Medicine Bibliography, 1639-1783*, Lathrop C. Harper, New York, (1962). Francis Packard, writing in 1931, thought Buchan's work had been used more than any other book of its kind ever had been and ever would be. It was an instant success, selling 80,000 copies in Buchan's lifetime and subsequently was translated in all major European languages (*Dictionary of National Biography*, III:180-181).

[2] Gunn, J.C., *Domestic Medicine*, (New York, NY: Saxton, Barker and Co., 1860), p. 141. Originally published in Knoxville in 1830, Gunn's work went through dozens of editions, by the ninth claiming over 100,000 in sales. See M.E. Pickard and R.C. Buley, *The Midwest Pioneer, His Ills, Cure, and Doctors* (Crawfordsville, IN: Banta, 1945).

healings documented in the New Testament. The *Book of Mormon* contained examples of healing by faith (see Alma 15:10 and 3 Nephi 17:8), and the Prophet Joseph Smith confirmed its efficacy (see D&C 35:9 and 46:19).

In addition to healing by faith and the common sense domestic medicine practiced by the early saints, there were two types of professional medical care available at the time. Some historians call the one Heroic Medicine and the other Botanic Medicine.

Judging by modern medical standards it is difficult to determine which was worse, though in retrospect Botanic Medicine did less harm.

BOTANIC MEDICINE

Although the two types of medical treatment were sometimes intermingled, Botanic Medicine was actually somewhere between Domestic Medicine and the mainstream Heroic Medicine (described below). Botanic medicine often became a part-time occupation that required neither licensing or special training.

The autobiography of one lay doctor suggests how easy it was to become a physician. In 1844 James Still, a free Negro in New Jersey, bought a book of "medical botany" and began to prepare medical remedies for his family. In return for some sassafras roots, he agreed to treat a neighbor who suffered from hemorrhoids.

He borrowed a mortar and a long stone to grind the herbs. According to Still, "having prepared the remedy, I took it to him, and it had the desired effect. In a few days he was well. I was pleased, and so was he. It did not occur to me at this time, however, that I was practicing medicine."[1] Though self-taught, James Still eventually took up healing as a practical vocation.

The 1822 book, *New Guide to Health*,[2] published by New Englander Samuel Thomson, created a society of botanic doctors. In 1809 Thomson had

---

[1] Still, J., *Early Recollections and Life of Dr. James Still*, (reprinted New Brunswick, NJ: Rutgers University Press, 1973), p. 77.

[2] Thomson, S., *Narrative of the Life and Medical Discoveries of Samuel Thomson*, to which is added, "An Introduction to his New Guide to Health," 2nd ed., (Boston, 1825).

obtained a patent from the federal government for his system of botanic medicine, enabling him to sell rights for use of his methods and to claim official endorsement. The book was used both by families and by Thomsonian practitioners. Thomson boasted that by 1839 he had sold 100,000 copies of his book and that one half of Ohio's population followed his teachings.

Herbs and "natural" remedies stood at the heart of the system. Many doctors, said Thomson, "have learned just enough to know how to deceive people, and keep them in ignorance, by covering their doings under a language unknown to their patients." He was referring to the mainstream heroic doctors with their indecipherable Latin nomenclature and their "elite" bearing.

HEROIC (MAINSTREAM) MEDICINE

As the War of 1812 drew to a close, medical schools proliferated in the United States. The schools generally had dubious beginnings; typically, a group of physicians approached a local college and proposed a school. Being able to affiliate with a school lent legitimacy to their enterprise and gave them the authority to grant degrees. The physicians were not the only ones who came out ahead: the college increased its prestige without any out-of-pocket costs (student tuition paid the expenses).

The physical facilities often consisted of only two rooms, one for lectures and one for dissections. There were no laboratories, and many had only limited libraries. Many students received a Bachelor of Medicine degree in only three or four months of study and, with the certificate from the medical school, began to practice medicine.

It was considered a great reform in several states when in 1850 two years of "graduated study" were required before students could earn a Doctor of Medicine degree and be licensed to practice medicine. "Graduated study" meant that students could not repeat the same courses during the second year. The school year usually lasted only three to four months—and those were in the winter—because students were needed at home for spring planting, summer cultivating, and fall harvesting.

These poorly trained medical practitioners were in some ways an extension of the English medical system. In England, a guild system had developed in which there were three classes: physicians, who were the elite; surgeons, who were craftsmen valued only slightly above a barber; and druggists, who were tradesmen who could dispense medication but could give no advice.[1]

Interestingly, the English physicians, as gentlemen, refused to work with their hands and only observed, speculated and prescribed. Doing otherwise would demean them. However, in the land of the rough and ready colonists with their ideas of freedom, there was little stratification of classes. Every man was free to follow his own dream. Many men practiced medicine part-time and pursued their usual vocation the rest of the time.

By 1833, medical science was scarcely in its infancy; it would be another forty years before scientific investigation and verification began to be applied to medicine. Although the renowned Louis Pasteur was living in France, he had not yet documented the germ theory. A Dutch scientist named Leeuwenhoek had invented the microscope, but it was only strong enough for him to detail the life cycle of a flea. A mysterious disease called "childbirth fever" (puerperal sepsis) still killed many women shortly after childbirth, the unknowing victims of unsanitary delivery and bacterial contamination.

Mainstream heroic medicine in 1833 advocated the harmful and scientifically unjustified practices of blood letting, skin blistering, leeching, and purging with harmful laxatives. Physicians prescribed opium to treat drinking problems.

Dangerous elixirs were being concocted by unregulated business ventures. Opium-based Brown's Teething Cordial was sold for fretful babies. As addiction to opium became a problem, cocaine became a favorite tonic ingredient.

It was in this setting that the magnificent Word of Wisdom was revealed—a law of health that can now be evaluated by today's scientific and medical evidence.

Initially, as the revelation states, the Word of Wisdom was given as a set of "principles" or guidelines with certain promises. A year later (1834), after

---

[1] Reader, W., *The Rise of the Professional Classes in Nineteenth Century England*, (New York, NY: Basic Books, Inc., 1966).

the prophet met with his recently organized High Council and discussed the question of adherence to this revelation with its health principles, the following decision was expressed and accepted unanimously by the High Council: "No official member in this Church is worthy to hold an office after having the word of wisdom properly taught him; and he, the official member, neglecting to comply with and obey it."[1]

This statement is one we need to face today. Have we been taught properly? Are we trying to understand and follow the food plan in this law even as we learn and teach one another truths documented by facts unknown just a few years ago?

---

[1] *History of the Church* (Salt Lake City, UT: Church of Jesus Christ of Latter-day Saints), vol. II, pp. 34-35.

CHAPTER TWO

MEDICINE AND MORMONISM (1833-1900)

Hyrum Smith, the prophet's older brother and closest friend, shared martyrdom with Joseph when they both were killed by assassin's bullets in Carthage, Illinois in 1844. Two years before his death, Hyrum, as Patriarch of the Church, gave a lengthy discourse on the Word of Wisdom.

After affirming that the principles in the scriptures are the work of God and are pure, Hyrum said,

> They are principles of righteousness; they are given for a blessing to the human family, and the salvation, temporal and spiritual, of his saints....When God first made man upon the earth, he was a different being entirely to what he now is; his body was strong, athletic, robust and healthy; his days were prolonged upon the earth; he lived nearly one thousand years, his mind was vigorous and active, and his intellectual faculties clear and comprehensive, but he has become degenerated; his life has dwindled to a span; disease preys upon his system; his body is enervated and feeble; and his ment[al] and intellectual faculties are impaired, and weakened; and man is not now that dignified, noble, majestic, honorable, and mighty being that he was when he first proce[e]ded from the hands of his maker. God... knows what course to pursue to restore mankind to their pristine excellency and primitive vigour, and health; and He has appointed the *Word of Wisdom* as one of the engines to bring about this thing, to *remove the beastly appetites, the murderous disposition and the vitiated taste of man; to restore his body and vigour, promote peace between him and the brute creation, and as one of the little wheels in God's designs*, to help to regulate the great machinery, which shall eventually revolutionize the earth, and bring about the restoration of all things.
>
> *The Lord has told us what is good for us to eat, and to drink, and what is pernicious*; but some of our wise philosophers, and some of our elders too, pay no regard to it; they think it too little, too foolish, for wise men to regard— fools! Where is their wisdom, philosophy and intelligence? From whence did they obtain their superior light?...They think it too small for him to

condes[c]end to tell men what will be nutritious or what will be unhealthy. Who made the corn, the wheat, the rye, and all the vegetable substances? And who was it that organized man, and constituted him as he is found? Who made his stomach, and his digestive organs, and prepared *proper nutriment* for his system, that the juices of his body might be supplied; and *his form be invigorated by that kind of food which the laws of nature, and the laws of God has said would be good for man?*...

...Listen not to the teaching of any man, or any elder who says the word of wisdom is of no moment;... Why is it that we are frequently so dull and languid? It is because we break the word of wisdom; disease preys upon our system, our understandings are darkened, and we do not comprehend the things of God; the devil takes advantage of us, and we fall into temptation... Be it remembered—that this instruction is given "in consequence of evils and designs that do and will exist in the heart of conspiring men in the last days...."

After quoting from the Word of Wisdom (D&C 89:10-15), Hyrum continued:

Let men attend to these instructions, let them use the things ordained of God; *let them be sparing of the life of animals; it is pleasing saith the Lord that flesh be used only in times of winter, or of famine*—and why to be used in famine? Because all domesticated animals would naturally die, and may as well be made use of by man, as not.

After quoting again from the Word of Wisdom (D&C 89:16-21), he exhorted his listeners:

Let these things be adhered to; let the saints be wise; let us lay aside our folly and abide by the commandments of God; so shall we be blessed of the great Jehovah in time and eternity; we shall be healthy, strong and vigorous: we shall be enabled to resist disease; and wisdom will crown our councils, and our bodies will become strong and powerful, our progeny will become mighty, and will rise up and call us blessed.... We shall prepare ourselves for the purposes of Jehovah[1] *(emphasis added)*

This discourse leaves no doubt what the pivotal word "sparingly" in D&C 89:12 meant to Hyrum Smith in 1842.

---

[1] *Times and Seasons* (Salt Lake City, UT: Church of Jesus Christ of Latter-day Saints) 3:799-801 (emphasis added).

The second president of the Church, Brigham Young, was only five years older than the Prophet Joseph Smith and undoubtedly survived the same childhood diseases. After bearing eleven children, his mother died of tuberculosis at a young age. Brigham's first wife, Miriam Works, died in 1832 of tuberculosis after giving birth to two children.

Like almost everyone living in Nauvoo in 1839, Brigham was stricken with malaria. Malaria was endemic in the Mississippi River area, and almost all residents sooner or later had their "seasoning," usually in their first summer when they were infected by the Anopheles mosquito. The Prophet contracted malaria at the same time as Brigham, but with characteristic charisma Joseph rose from his sick bed to heal others. Even though he was also ill with malaria, Brigham was helped by a blessing and accompanied the Prophet to comfort other victims of the disease.

Two months later Brigham was still not well and wrote that his health was so poor that he "was unable to go thirty rods to the river without assistance." Three months later he was still "unable to sit up," but nevertheless departed on a mission to England, being "fitted up" in a wagon. When he later reached England he was so emaciated that his cousin, Willard Richards, did not recognize him.

Three years later, having returned to Nauvoo, Brigham Young was stricken with severe scarlet fever. Ill for eighteen days, he had a sudden cardiac arrest which responded to mouth-to-mouth resuscitation by his wife.

In an 1855 discourse, Brigham referred to his earlier illnesses as he counseled the Saints "to lay the foundation for a healthy posterity." As he noted, we are to prepare to live instead of preparing to die, for he said,

> The fathers and mothers have laid the foundation for many of these diseases, from generation to generation, until the people are reduced to their present condition. True, some live to from fifty to ninety years of age, but it is an unusual circumstance to see a man a hundred years old, or a woman ninety. *The people have laid the foundation of short life through their diet,* their rest, their labor, and their doing this, that, and the other in a wrong manner, with improper motives, and at improper times.
>
> I would be glad to tell mothers how to lay the foundation of health in their children, that they may be delivered from the diseases with which I am afflicted, and have been from my youth up...some say that "this is a miserable world, I do not care how soon I get through." Well, go and destroy yourselves,

if you choose; you have all the opportunity that you can desire; there is plenty of arsenic, calomel, and other means, within your reach... Latter-day Saints who live merely to get ready to die are not worth much; *rather get ready to live, and be prepared to live to the glory of your Father in Heaven and to do the work He has given you to do.*[1] *(emphasis added)*

As will be pointed out later in this book, today we could substitute the words "fat" and "cholesterol" for Brigham's words "arsenic" and "calomel." There's one big difference, though: in his time, arsenic and calomel were ingested out of ignorance. Today, we eat animal fat and cholesterol not in ignorance, but because of self-indulgent rationalization.

The commonsense approach of using one's heart and head concerning the Word of Wisdom was discussed by Apostle George Q. Cannon who said in a 1867 discourse,

There should be a well settled conviction in the mind of every person belonging to this Church that it would be a real benefit for him or her to observe the Word of Wisdom, and carry into effect the counsel God has given on any point. If I do not see the evils that result from...*eating meats to excess*, and the benefits that would result from abstaining, what anybody else may see would only have a temporary effect upon me. I must feel in my own heart that it is injurious to me to indulge in these things; there must be a well settled conviction within me that this is the case.[2] *(emphasis added)*

In 1868, another discourse by Apostle Cannon was an attempt to wade through the misinformation of those times. He said,

The greatest boon that God has given us, and that upon which every other hinges, is life. *With life we need health, the power to carry out designs of our beings upon the earth.* We are told that swine's flesh is not good, and that we should dispense with it; and *we are told that flesh of any kind is not suitable to man in the summer time, and ought to eaten sparingly in the winter.* The question arises... "What then are we to eat if we drop swine's flesh and eat very little beef or mutton...why, dear me, we shall starve to death." In conversation with one of the brethren the other day, the brother remarked "the diet of the

[1] *Journal of Discourses* (Salt Lake City, UT: Church of Jesus Christ of Latter-day Saints), 2:269-71 (emphasis added).

[2] *Journal of Discourses* 12:44-45 (emphasis added).

poor is principally bread and meat, and if they dispense with meat, they will be reduced to very hard fare." I reasoned with him...that other articles of food could be raised more cheaply and in greater variety than the flesh of animals.... We as a people should turn our attention to the multiplication of varieties of food in our midst. We should not confine ourselves to a few articles of diet....It is an exceedingly difficult thing for most people to break off and discontinue cherished and long standing habits...we can have a *variety in diet*, and yet have simplicity. We can have a diet that will be easily prepared, and yet have it *healthful*. We can have a diet, that will be *tasteful*, *nutritious* and *delightful* to us, and *easy to digest*; and yet not wear out the lives of our mothers, wives, daughters and sisters in its preparation.[1] *(emphasis added)*

First Counselor to President Wilford Woodruff in 1892, Elder Cannon's counsel still applies today:

Our religion impresses upon us the importance of taking care of our bodies. *There is a carelessness and an indifference even among us that are not found among many well-informed people in the world.* Many of the Saints do not seem to be alive to the importance of those laws which pertain to well-being and preservation of the health and strength of the body. Their old traditions cling to them...*Pestilence[s] of various kinds* which we are led to expect through the word of the Lord are *yet to break forth, [and] will have their effect in calling the Saints' attention to those laws of life and health.*

Elder Cannon continues,

This revealed Word of Wisdom embodies the most advanced principles of science in the condemnation of unclean or gluttonous appetites; and if it were implicitly obeyed by the human family, it would be a power to aid in a physical redemption for the race.[2] *(emphasis added)*

It is interesting to note that Apostle Cannon said, "pestilence[s] of various kinds...are yet to break forth." As will be pointed out in this book, we have largely rid ourselves of infectious pestilence; in a very real sense, today's pestilences are heart attacks, strokes and cancer.

---

[1] *Journal of Discourses* 12: 12:221-224 (emphasis added).

[2] *Juvenile Instructor* 27 (May 15, 1892): pp. 690-91. See also: Newquist, *Gospel Truth* (Salt Lake City, UT: Deseret Book, 1974), 2:175.

Eliza R. Snow was the most fascinating and dominant Mormon woman in the nineteenth century. Baptized in 1835, she became the wife of two prophets and was the sister of a third. Among her many accomplishments, she wrote the words for ten lovely hymns that still appear in LDS song books today. One of the hymns, "In Our Lovely Deseret,"[1] was written more than a hundred years ago, but carries a vital message for us today. The second verse reads,

> That the children may live long,
> And be beautiful and strong,
> Tea and coffee and tobacco they despise,
> Drink no liquor, and *they eat*
> *But a very little meat;*
> They are seeking to be great and good and wise. *(emphasis added)*

How often do we and our children sing this hymn with gusto, but fail to obey one of its tenets?

Eliza's brother, Apostle Lorenzo Snow, discussed the Word of Wisdom in a meeting of the First Presidency and the Quorum of the Twelve in May, 1893. After reading D&C 89:10-16 and drawing "special attention to that part which relates to the use of meat, which he considered just as strong as that which related to the use of liquors and hot drinks," Apostle Snow "was convinced that the killing of animals when unnecessary was wrong and sinful, and that it was not right to neglect one part of the Word of Wisdom and be too strenuous in regard to other parts."[2]

In an 1897 meeting of the First Presidency and the Quorum of the Twelve in the Salt Lake Temple, Apostle Snow

> ...introduced the subject of the Word of Wisdom, expressing the opinion that it was violated as much or more in the improper use of meat as in other things, and thought *the time was near at hand when the Latter-day Saints should be*

---

[1] *Hymns of the Church of Jesus Christ of Latter-day Saints* (Salt Lake City, UT: Church of Jesus Christ of Latter-day Saints, 1985), Hymn 307.

[2] *Journal History*, 5 May 1893, pp. 2-3.

taught to refrain from meat eating and the shedding of animal blood.[1]
(emphasis added)

Apostle Snow became the fifth president of the church in 1898.

---

[1] *Journal History,* 11 March 1897, p. 2.

CHAPTER THREE

MEDICINE AND MORMONISM (1900-1950)

President Lorenzo Snow died in 1901 and was succeeded by President Joseph F. Smith, the son of Hyrum Smith. As the twentieth century began, Mormondom was largely an isolated community of converts who had left their homes in Europe and the eastern United States to live in "Zion," the Rocky Mountains. It would be another forty-seven years before church membership would reach one million, and ninety-two years before it would reach eight million.

Medical care in the United States was beginning to be based on medical science, which had made enormous advances during the previous two decades. In "Zion," however, Saints were still skeptical toward physicians—a skepticism based on experiences with the Heroic Medicine practiced in the 1800s before the Mormon exodus to the Salt Lake Valley.

The Saints still remembered the words of Brigham Young to the soldiers of the Mormon Battalion when they prepared to serve in the U.S. Army against Mexico. He wrote:

> If you are sick, live by faith, and let the surgeon's medicine alone if you want to live, using only such herbs and mild food as are at your disposal.[1]

His prejudice against doctors was emphasized in another statement, in which he said of physicians "A worse set of ignoramuses do not walk the earth."[2] He felt that useful and true medical knowledge should be available to all, and those unwilling to share their knowledge were "corrupt." In an

---

[1] Clark, J., *Messages of the First Presidency* (Salt Lake City, UT: Church of Jesus Christ of Latter-day Saints), 1:302.

[2] Wilcox, L., "The Imperfect Science: Brigham Young on Medical Doctors," *Dialogue* 12:30 (1979).

apparent shift of opinion, he later did send several members of the Church to the eastern United States for medical training.

The Saints in Brigham Young's time were living beyond this country's frontiers, and medical advances were slow to arrive. By 1900, the Salt Lake Valley area hosted a large non-Mormon population, mostly ex-U.S. Army personnel, gold seekers, and immigrants who settled in the area. Several non-Mormon doctors stayed in Utah after their discharge from the Army; because of friction between Mormons and non-Mormons over political issues, non-Mormon doctors were often considered "anti-Mormon."

As the Saints of the period struggled to live the tenets of the Word of Wisdom, they also were instructed by church leaders concerning their relationship to God's "brute creations."

The moral issue of killing animals was commented on by the sixth president of the Church, Joseph F. Smith, when in 1913 he said:

> *I do not believe any man should kill animals or birds unless he "needs" them for food....*I think it is wicked for men to thirst in their souls to kill almost everything which possesses animal life. It is wrong, and I have been surprised at prominent men whom I have seen whose very souls seemed to be athirst for the shedding of animal blood. They go off hunting deer, antelope, elk, anything they can find, and what for? "Just for the fun of it!" I am a firm believer...in the simple words of one of the poets:
>
> Take not away the life you cannot give,
> For all things have an equal right to live.[1] *(emphasis added)*

In a statement later quoted by two other prophets, Smith taught that our relationships with nature are akin to our relationship with God:

> We are a part of life and should study carefully our relationship to it. We should be in sympathy with it, and not allow our prejudices to create a desire for its destruction. The unnecessary destruction of life begets a spirit of destruction which grows within the soul. It lives by what it feeds upon and robs man of the love that he should have for the works of God. It hardens the heart of man and makes him prey upon the social welfare which he should feel for the happiness and advancement of his fellowman. The unnecessary destruction

---

[1] Joseph F. Smith, "The Destruction of Animal Life," *Juvenile Instructor*, 48:309 (1913).

of life is a distinct spiritual loss to the human family. Men can not worship the Creator and look with careless indifference upon his creation. The love of all life helps man to the enjoyment of a better life. It exalts the spiritual nature of those in need of divine favor....Love of nature is akin to the love of God; the two are inseparable.[1]

This strong statement needs no reinforcement, but does bring to mind another powerful account, a conversation between Socrates and his friend, Glaucon some 2400 years ago.[2] Concerned with man's basic needs in contrast to man's excessive cravings, Socrates told of the consequences a group of people could expect when they ate a simple vegetarian diet: "And with such a diet they may be expected to live in peace and health to a good old age, and bequeath a similar life to their children."

Glaucon responds by telling Socrates that people will not be satisfied by a simple diet, and will want to eat "pig's flesh." Socrates answers that people should avoid things "not required by natural need." He then describes a group of people with greater wants than needs. This group or society requires *more physicians, more land and will go to war to get what they want.* Let's review their conversation:

> Socrates: "And there will be animals of many kinds, if people eat them?"
> Glaucon: "Certainly."
> Socrates: "And living in this way, we shall have much greater need of physicians then before?"
> Glaucon: "Much greater."
> Socrates: "And the country which was enough to support the original inhabitants will be too small now, and not enough?"
> Glaucon: "Quite true."
> Socrates: "Then a slice of our neighbor's land will be wanted by us for pasture and tillage, and they will want a slice of ours, if, like ourselves, they exceed the limit of necessity and give themselves up to the unlimited accumulation of wealth?"
> Glaucon: "That, Socrates, will be inevitable."
> Socrates: "And so we shall go to war, Glaucon, shall we not?"

---

[1] Joseph F. Smith, quoted in Gerald Jones, *Concern for Animals as Manifest in Five American Churches*, Ph.D. diss., Brigham Young University (1972), pp. 107-8.

[2] Plato, *The Republic*, Brittanica Great Books, Book II, p. 318.

A second and personal account that occurred years ago gives some food for thought. It illustrates the manner in which one accepts and responds to teachings of church leaders by changing one's lifestyle.

In a 1961 church magazine, *The Improvement Era*, was a discussion entitled "Is It a Sin to Kill Animals Wantonly?" written by Apostle Joseph Fielding Smith, then president of the Council of the Twelve, concerning man's relationship to animals.[1] One church member, a friend of mine and an avid hunter at that time, read the article and immediately stopped hunting. He, without fanfare, began to pursue other interests. I and a few others discussed the article and at the time thought it to be "meddling." Changing a lifestyle comes hard for some of us.

During the early 1900s while Joseph F. Smith was president of the Church, mainstream medicine came of age. Scientific advances of the late 1800s were translated into measures for the public's better health. The United States began to develop proper sewage control, water purification, quarantine for contagious disease, aseptic surgery, and some effective medications. The American Medical Association—structurally weak, disorganized, and racked with dissension since its beginning sixty years earlier—played little or no role in shaping early American medicine. But things were about to change.

In 1903 the American Medical Association adopted a revised code of ethics that, under a new constitution, tended to heal the schism among different types of practitioners. The AMA became a confederation of state medical societies, which in turn became a confederation of local county medical societies. In a remarkably short time physicians began to achieve a unity that had eluded them for sixty years. The membership of the AMA grew from 8,000 in 1900 to 70,000 by 1910, which included half of all the nation's physicians. This "federalization" was similar to that occurring in labor unions, trade associations, and corporations that were rapidly emerging in other fields.

In 1904, the AMA created a Council on Medical Education that began grading the 160 medical schools throughout the country according to three classes. After inspecting them, the council in 1906 fully approved 82 schools and gave them a "Class A" rating. "Class B" consisted of 46 schools,

---

[1] Joseph F. Smith, "Is it a sin to kill wantonly?" *Improvement Era*, (August 1961), p. 568.

considered imperfect but redeemable. The 32 "Class C" schools were deemed beyond salvage.

Interestingly, the results of this report were disclosed in an AMA meeting, but the report was never published.[1]

THE FLEXNER REPORT
BULLETIN NUMBER FOUR

Probably the single greatest impact on medicine in more than half a century was a 1910 report by Abraham Flexner, a young educator with a recent degree from Johns Hopkins University.[2] The AMA Council on Medical Education, through the auspices of the Carnegie Foundation, asked Flexner to accompany the AMA Council Secretary on a visit to each of the nation's medical schools. As a layman, his judgment on each school was reported in Bulletin Number Four.

Flexner's deft report clearly revealed deficiencies in some of the medical schools. The weaker medical school's catalogues were patently false; the extolled "laboratories" consisted only of a few test tubes in a cigar box; corpses reeked from inadequate disinfectant; tuition money, not academic skill, was the criterion for admission; and alleged faculty members were absent because of their busy private practice. As Flexner saw and documented, there was a great discrepancy between scientific/medical knowledge and its dissemination through medical education.

While science had progressed, the facilities for medical education had lagged behind. America had a few of the world's best—and many of the world's worst—medical schools. The country was oversupplied with badly trained doctors. Flexner's Bulletin Number Four and more stringent licensing of medical schools caused many schools to go out of business. By 1915 the

---

[1] Starr, P., *The Social Transformation of American Medicine*, (New York: Basic Books, Inc.), p. 118.

[2] Flexner, A. "Medical Education in the United States and Canada," Bulletin No. 4, New York: Carnegie Foundation (1910).

number of medical schools fell from 131 to 95, and the number of graduates from 5,440 to 3,535. Many state legislatures stepped in to provide needed financial support; under the aegis of universities and colleges, the control of medical education shifted from private medical practice to the academic climate of today. This change produced a medical profession whose knowledge was based on scientific verification.

The patent medicine industry was an area of unbridled exploitation in the 1800s but was controlled in the early 1900s. Bayer, the aspirin company, had marketed a cough syrup in 1898 that contained heroin; in the early 1900s, it was taken off the market. Even early Coca-Cola™ contained cocaine (hence its name). Cocaine was outlawed as a medication in 1915.

When medical care became based on science, physicians could offer rational explanations for many diseases—a situation that spelled disaster for unfounded nostrums and potions. In an effort to "legitimize" all proprietary medicines, the AMA began a successful campaign that forced manufacturers to disclose all ingredients. A campaign to stop misleading advertising of these remedies was not as successful. However, the nostrum-makers gradually lost credibility as the public began to rely on the medical profession for authoritative advice.

In 1903 the *Ladies Home Journal* warned about imprudent self-medication.[1] Editor Edward Bok pointed to powders and syrups containing opium, cocaine, and alcohol that unsuspecting mothers used themselves or gave their children. He wrote, "The physician's fee of a dollar or two, which the mother seeks to save, may prove to be the costliest form of economy which she has ever practiced."

These editorial warnings may seem ironic, considering that the magazine also carried an advertisement in 1905 showing a well-dressed woman, saying, "Try a little Tonic, and it's so much better than a drug of any kind." Since the Tonic of the day was basically alcohol, the ad message was clear. Cocaine, heroin and other narcotics were now unsavory—but alcohol was acceptable.

---

[1] Bok, E., "The Patent Medicine Curse," *Ladies Home Journal*, May 1903, pp. 21-18.

THE DENMARK STORY

World War I became the world's concern in 1914, and a remarkable story[1] from that period has great implications for us, even today.

Dr. Martin Hindhede, chairman of the Danish Institute of Nutrition, had become convinced by previous research that a vegetarian-type diet would be beneficial for human health. He also knew that meat production required large quantities of grains and other plant foods. (Today we know that the production of one pound of meat protein requires six to ten pounds of plant protein.)[2]

Under a land and sea blockade by the Germans, Denmark could import no grains to support meat production, and its people were faced with severe food shortages. Dr. Hindhede convinced the Danes to embark on a large nutritional experiment that required a drastic change in the foods they ate. They slaughtered 80 percent of their hogs and 34 percent of their dairy cows. The grain that had previously been used to feed hogs and cattle became the major part of a new diet for the Danish people.

They started producing "war bread" from whole rye flour with 15 percent wheat and wheat bran. Until the war ended, each person by governmental decree was allowed a daily allowance of *"very little meat"* and *small amounts of butter and milk*. The main dietary staple was *potatoes, cereals, and vegetables*. Alcohol was forbidden, and no tea, coffee or tobacco were available. In essence, the large-scale Danish experiment observed all tenets of the Word of Wisdom.

The diet was low-meat, low-protein, low-cholesterol, low-fat and high-fiber.

Within a matter of weeks, the benefits of the Danes' new food plan was apparent. During the year from October 1917 to October 1918 when food restrictions were the most severe, the death rate from disease had dropped over 34% from the average of the preceding 18 years. It was the lowest ever

---

[1] Hindhede M., "Die Neue Ernaehrungslehre," (1923); also Hindhede M., *Fuldkommen Sundhed* (1934); "The Effect of Food Restriction During War on Mortality in Copenhagen," *JAMA*, 74:381, (1920).

[2] Lappe, F., *Diet For A New Planet* (New York, NY: Ballantine Books, 1982); Altschul, A., *Proteins: Their Chemistry and Politics* (Nw York, NY: Basic Books, Inc., 1965).

known in Europe. Furthermore, Denmark was the only nation in Europe not to have a significant rise in the death rate as a consequence of the 1917 influenza epidemic. That statistic gives additional credence to recent evidence that a plant-centered diet increases immunity to infectious disease.

The Danish experiment vividly illustrates the waste that occurs when grains are cycled through livestock. As John Robbins points out in *Diet For a New America*,[1] animal production wastes 90 percent of the grain's protein, 96 percent of its calories, 100 percent of its fiber, and 100 percent of its carbohydrates.

In the years that followed, nutritional scientists began to study the effect of the consumption of animal products on health and disease. Mountains of data are now available to show this relationship.

As the science of nutrition progressed during the first half of the twentieth century, the LDS population continued to grow. Most Church converts emigrated to Zion in Utah.

During the leadership of seventh LDS church President Heber J. Grant, from 1918 to 1945, scientists first began to realize that tobacco was a deadly habit. President Grant was a strong proponent of the Word of Wisdom, preaching frequently about the revelation's ban on alcohol, tobacco, tea, and coffee.

He was also concerned about the food plan in of the Word of Wisdom. In 1925, President Grant exclaimed that;

> No man who breaks the Word of Wisdom can gain the same amount of knowledge and intelligence in this world as the man who obeys that law. I don't care who he is or where he comes from, his mind will not be as clear, and he cannot advance as far and as rapidly and retain his power as much as he would if he obeyed the Word of Wisdom.[2]

Twelve years later he said,

> I think that another reason I have very splendid strength for an old man is that during the years we have had a cafeteria in the Utah Hotel *I have not, with*

---

[1] Robbins, J., *Diet For a New America* (Walpole, NH: Still Publishing, 1987).

[2] Grant, H., *Conference Report* (Salt Lake City, UT: Church of Jesus Christ of Latter-day Saints, April 1925), p. 10.

the exception of not more than a dozen times, ordered meat of any kind. On these special occasions I have mentioned I have perhaps had a small tender lamb chop. *I have endeavored to live the Word of Wisdom and that, in my opinion, is one reason for my good health.*[1]

President Grant's statement about breaking the Word of Wisdom is similar to one made by his contemporary, film producer Cecil B. DeMille, who said, "The history of mankind has shown us, we cannot break God's laws, rather we break ourselves against them."

President Grant died just before the end of World War II in 1945. Ezra Taft Benson, then an apostle, traveled to Europe to assess the postwar damage and determine the needs of the starving Saints.[2]

The first statistics that caught my medical attention as a young doctor were the death rates of Europeans under Nazi occupation during and after the war. The graph on the next page shows that during the Nazi occupation, deaths from heart disease, strokes, and other circulatory diseases dropped dramatically in Norway.[3] Caloric intake was low; no one was fat. Despite hunger and stress, these people were protected from fatal strokes and heart attacks. As soon as the war ended, milk, eggs, and meat became available, and the death rates rose to pre-war levels.

When President George Albert Smith became the eighth president of the LDS Church in 1945, it seems clear that he made choices about his food habits that relate to the Word of Wisdom. His son-in-law recorded, "In the summer he eats no meat, and even in the winter months he eats very little."[4]

In 1950, Apostle John A. Widtsoe and his wife, Leah, published a book, *The Word of Wisdom, A Modern Interpretation.*[5] Learned and well esteemed, Apostle Widtsoe was a Norwegian immigrant and Harvard graduate. In the light of today's knowledge his book deserves review and comment.

---

[1] Grant, H., *Conference Report* (Salt Lake City, UT: Church of Jesus Christ of Latter-day Saints, April 1937), p. 15.

[2] Benson, E., *A Labor of Love* (Salt Lake City, UT: Deseret Book Co., 1989).

[3] Malmos, H., "The Relation of Nutrition to Health," *Acta Med. Scand.*, (1950).

[4] Quoted in Gerald E. Jones, *Concern for Animals as Manifest in Five American Churches: Bible Christian, Shaker, Latter-day Saint, Christian Scientist and Seventh-Day Adventist,* Ph.D. diss., Brigham Young University (1972), p. 111.

[5] Widtsoe, J and L., *The Word of Wisdom, A Modern Interpretation* (Salt Lake City, UT: Deseret Book,1950).

Interestingly, it never mentions the word *cholesterol* and mentions the word *fiber* only a few times. Of course, most facts about cholesterol and fiber were not known in 1950. Today they are the "buzz words" in the news and health media.

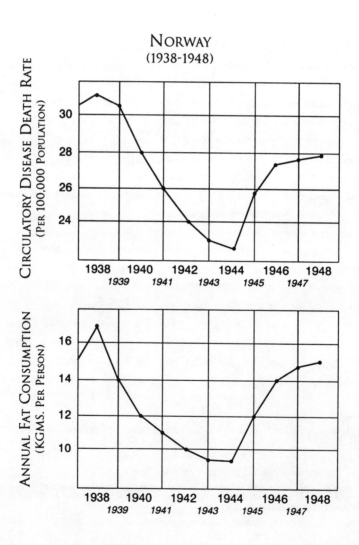

Widtsoe's book came under some unjust criticism because of his indictment of white flour. His indictment was based on the fact that in 1950 the white flour was stripped of most of its vitamins, minerals, and protein. Now we know that the refinement process also strips flour of its fiber. Today's "enriched" white flour is supplemented with added nutrients, but is still missing the fiber.

Forty years ago when Widtsoe sought the truth, he relied on faith in the Word of Wisdom revelation. He wrote in his book:

> Conflicts may appear between the teaching of science and the Word of Wisdom.... The Food and Nutrition Committee of the National Research Council recommends meat daily; but the Word of Wisdom says definitely [eat] meat sparingly and then only in winter or famine. *In time the scientist will prove that the teaching of the inspired Word is correct and until then it may be relied on as a safe guide....* To date, nothing has been discovered to set at naught any truth taught in the Word of Wisdom, and if we may judge by the past, all statements made therein will in time be proved true. *(emphasis added)*

Many of the things that Widtsoe wrote have been confirmed by subsequent medical and scientific studies.

The following, in his own words, gives us a challenge for modern living:

> It was shown early in the history of plant science that plants contain all of the necessary food substances: proteins, fats, starches and other carbohydrates, minerals and water. Later it was discovered that the plant kingdom is the best source of the sixth necessary group of food substances, vitamins.
>
> The great Builder of the earth provided well for the physical needs of His children. Countless varieties of edible plants, vegetables, cereals, fruits and nuts are yielded by Mother Nature for man's daily food. Some furnish one predominating food element, some another, each filling some need of the human structure, as bricks in a wall, or as promoters of proper metabolism, to secure his health.
>
> Man should partake in plenty of all edible fruits and vegetables. It is a mistake for a normal person to say: "I don't like this vegetable or that," and refuse to eat it. Children should be taught...to eat and enjoy all the different kinds of vegetables so that their bodies may grow in bone strength and nerve tone as well as in size. This practice should be encouraged in adults as well, for all have need of the nutritive value of fruits and vegetables.

Most fruits should be eaten raw, fully ripe, and "in the season thereof." Fruits and vegetables should be eaten in liberal amounts by young and old, and with grain products should form the bulk of the human dietary.

If one uses meat it must be used sparingly and in winter or famine only, as stated in this wise *law of health*. They who wish to be well and gain the promised reward stated in the Word of Wisdom must obey all of the law, not just part of it as suits their whim or their appetite, or their notion of its meaning.

...The foods used by many careless or uninformed modern civilized people yield a shortage, in greater or lesser degree, of many necessary food factors, especially of vitamins and minerals. This is because so much of the food of so-called civilized man today is preserved, salted, sugared, purified, polished, pickled, canned, extracted, distilled, concentrated, heated, dried, frozen, thawed, stored, packaged, processed and refined! ...The Word of Wisdom warns against the "evils and designs which do and will exist in the hearts of conspiring men in the last days."

If prudence is knowledge applied to daily need, then one with an intelligent interest in food and good life habits is in no sense a faddist or "crank." Indeed, every one should have such a sound fundamental knowledge of nutrition.

The most ardent Word of Wisdom enthusiasts cannot claim that this inspired document gives the last detailed word in nutritional advice. *Scientific knowledge concerning man's diet is yet in its infancy.* Many new angles to old truths are being discovered constantly. When such are definitely established in the best laboratories of nutrition to be facts, not mere theories, then they may be accepted and used and they will be found to be in harmony with the general principles set forth by the Word of Wisdom. The advice in the Word of Wisdom *to use prudence in all these things implies that one should be ready to accept and apply new truth.*"[1] *(emphasis added)*

It has been more than forty years since the above words were written by Apostle Widtsoe, who brought into clear focus the spiritual reality of the Word of Wisdom and its relation to the medical and scientific truth of that time.

---

[1] Widtsoe, J and L., *The Word of Wisdom, A Modern Interpretation* (Salt Lake City, UT: Deseret Book,1950).

CHAPTER FOUR

MEDICINE AND MORMONISM (1950 TO PRESENT)

When President George Albert Smith died in 1951, Second Counselor David O. McKay became president of the LDS Church. The Korean War was several months old; I had been called into the Army Medical Corps and in 1952 the U.S. Army sent me to Korea at a time of heavy fighting. There I learned a valuable Word of Wisdom lesson.

As a team of doctors using a primitive artificial kidney machine, we were able to save about half the American and Korean soldiers who developed acute kidney failure as a consequence of severe battle wounds.[1] In autopsies of the soldiers who died, the difference between the American and Korean soldiers was very apparent.

Autopsy studies on Korean soldiers showed no evidence of early atherosclerosis, the beginning of heart disease. They were protected from the ravages of atherosclerosis by their plant-centered diet, low in fat and cholesterol. But even the young American soldiers showed early evidence of the disease; in fact, the disease was far advanced in some of the them.[2] With today's knowledge, it is clear that the American diet containing excess fat and cholesterol was the offender.

We now live in the age of magic antibiotics, the eradication of polio, the miracle of organ transplants, and the power of artificial kidneys. We have wonderful diagnostic and therapeutic tools whose names are so long that we identify them only with initials. Medical knowledge has grown by leaps and bounds, yet we are still dying prematurely. Why? Because we as a nation and as individuals have not taken the steps to prevent premature death. Perhaps

---

[1] Teschan, P., et al., "Post-traumatic Renal Insufficiency in Military Casualties," I., *Am. J. Med.*, 18:172-186 (February 1955); II., *Am. J. Med.*, 18:187-204 (February 1955).

[2] Enos, W., "Pathogenesis of Coronary Disease in American Soldiers Killed in Korea," *JAMA*, 158:912, (1955).

someday a diet of excess fat and cholesterol will be looked upon as we now look upon tobacco and alcohol.

In an article in the "Church News" section of the *Deseret News*, Dr. Ted Adams, Director, Fitness Institute, Division of Cardiology, LDS Hospital, states, "We all want good health! Very few possessions ever equal the gift of good health."[1] He recommends maintaining exercise, as well as reducing fats, simple sugars and sodium in the food, getting proper sleep, proper skin care, taking good care of teeth and gums, avoiding substance abuse, changing the type of food to maintain a proper body weight and scheduling periodic medical checkups.

All of these generalities are good, but I should like you to focus on the food recommendations. They are: reducing fats and simple sugars in food and changing the type of food to maintain a proper body weight. If the 1988 statement by Surgeon General Koop that 68% of all deaths in the United States are diet-related is correct, the most important focus on our lifestyle should be on our diet. What we eat largely determines whether we have good health or die prematurely of preventable disease.

During the first half of the twentieth century, the United States made enormous strides in the health of individuals because prevention programs were developed and put in place. The U.S. Public Health Service programs were noteworthy. There were immunization programs, quarantines for communicable disease, programs to eradicate mosquito-borne disease, water sanitation and fluoridation treatment programs.

Gradually, however, certain miracles of treatment became medical celebrities: first insulin, then thyroid and other hormones, then antibiotics. These injections and pills, along with hundreds of other therapies, became the leading edge of medicine. We thought that with enough money spent on research and development we could solve today's health problems. The focus became treatment, not prevention.

Unfortunately, money cannot buy everything. Affluence has even made our health problems worse. The countries too poor to produce or import animal products do not have the degenerative diseases that plague the Western world. Preventable heart disease takes a terrible toll in money and lost lives.

---

[1] Adams, T. M.D., "We largely control our well-being," *Deseret News* "Church News" section, December 26, 1992.

One man in nine now develops prostate cancer. One woman in eight now develops breast cancer, and the statistics for both cancer of the prostate and breast are worsening each year.

Yet we still hope for the quick fix. A huge industry now spends millions of dollars to fashion magic bullets against chronic and deadly degenerative diseases. Sound noble? It might be, except for the fact that they don't work and we already have the knowledge to prevent many of these medical problems. The answer doesn't involve a pill or a quick fix. What it involves is a different food plan.

A recent series of six nationally published newspaper articles gives some insight into our "medical-pharmacologic" effort and the expenditure of taxpayer money. Take a look at some of the expensive research programs you are funding with your state and federal tax dollars:

1. At the University of Wisconsin, researchers are studying the adrenal hormone DHEA (dehydroepiandosterone) for its ability to preserve youth. Injections of DHEA are being given to animals and even a few humans.

2. Scientists at Temple University and other universities are studying DHEA as well as two other hormones, thymosin and melatonin, as the search for anti-aging chemicals continues.

3. A geneticist at the University of Colorado now reports that by changing one gene involved in oxygen metabolism he is able to increase the three-week life span of a round worm by 110 percent. One overly enthusiastic science reporter explained that "the gene involved in oxygen metabolism turned into a frenzied ninja that attacked free radical molecules."

4. The U.S. Department of Agriculture's Human Nutrition Research Center on Aging, located at Tufts University in Boston, evaluates more than two thousand people each year. Research subjects are housed in a dormitory-like facility and paid a small wage while they are studied.

A similar study is underway at the Baltimore National Institute on Aging.

5. The National Cancer Institute in Bethesda, Maryland has used taxpayer money to fund twenty-one research centers for the study of organic compounds with such unlikely names as limonoids, glucarates, phenolic acids, flavonoids, coumarins, polyacetylenes, and carotenoids. They are searching

for what appear to be strong anti-cancer compounds in plants such as garlic, licorice root, flaxseed, citrus fruit, carrots, celery, and parsley.

6. "Free radicals" and "anti-oxidants" are the new buzz words in the anti-cancer industry. The National Institutes of Health had launched an unprecedented five-year study involving more than 40,000 women but it was canceled because of compliance problems. It was a $17 million study that was designed to identify the role of vitamin E and beta carotene, both anti-oxidants that researchers theorize might prevent cancer and heart disease.

7. Roche, the world's largest vitamin producer, is building a multi-million dollar plant that will produce 350 tons of beta carotene per year. That's enough to supply every American adult with one daily 50 mg capsule—or the equivalent of seven large carrots. Does every adult in America need the equivalent of seven large carrots each day? No one knows, but you'll soon see advertising for it.

All this research is expensive and time-consuming—and is particularly questionable when we already have so many answers. Instead of spending our money on pills and extensive research, we should use it to educate ourselves and our children about a food plan that can prevent disease.

Researchers already know that people in countries with diets that consist almost entirely of locally grown fruits and vegetables are protected against cancer and heart disease.[1] In America, on the other hand, where fresh produce represents only a small part of our diet, cancer and heart disease are the most frequent causes of death.[2] Those facts should cause us to question our priorities—and question where our limited research monies should be spent.

Inspired Church leaders have practiced and taught the principles in the Word of Wisdom. President David O. McKay, ninth president of the LDS Church, often urged members of the church to live all the tenets of the Word of Wisdom.

---

[1] Campbell, C., A Study on Diet, Nutrition and Disease in the People's Republic of China, Division of Nutritional Sciences, (Ithaca, NY: Cornell University, 1990).

[2] Freeman, H., "Dietary Fibre and Colonic Neoplasia," Can. Med. Assoc., 121:291-296, (1979) ; Burkitt, D., "Colon-Rectal Cancer: Fiber and Other Dietary Factors," Am. J. Clin. Nut., 31:558-564, (1978); Cummings, J., "Dietary Fibre and Large Bowel Cancer," Proc. Nutr. Soc., 40:7-14, (1981); Armstrong, B., "Diet and Reproductive Hormones: A Study of Vegetarian and Omnivorous Women," JNCI, 67:761-767, (1981); Hirayama, T. "Epidemioloby of Breast Cancer with Special Reference to the Role of Diet," Prev. Med., 7:73-75, (1978); Campbell, T., A Study on Diet, Nutrition and Disease in the People's Republic of China, Division of Nutritional Sciences, (Ithaca, NY: Cornell University,1990).

Too many members move along the lines of least resistance," he said, "and yield to a craving appetite developed by disobedience to the Word of Wisdom of God, thus depriving themselves of spiritual as well as physical strength... Neither the Church nor the world at large can hear too much about the Word of Wisdom.... It is [the] courageous living of our lives in harmony with our ideals.... With the ideals of right living before him, no Latter-day Saint can continually violate the Word of Wisdom with impunity.[1]

It is recorded that the tenth president of the LDS Church, Joseph Fielding Smith, had a "disdain of meat and [a] love of vegetables." As his wife reported, "my husband doesn't eat meat," but rather "lots of fruit and vegetables."[2]

In his book *Teachings of the Prophet Joseph Smith*, President Joseph Fielding Smith recorded our first prophet's words:

This is the principle on which the government of heaven is conducted—by revelation adapted to the circumstances in which the children of the kingdom are placed. Whatever God requires is right, no matter what it is, although we may not see the *reason* thereof till long after the *events* transpire.[3] *(emphasis added)*

The Word of Wisdom was given to us 160 years ago. Today, with recent medical "events," we can see the "reason" for the Word of Wisdom. It has been given to us in the last days and is carefully adapted to the circumstances in which we live.

In language that is plain to everyone, President Ezra Taft Benson has given several strong messages about the Word of Wisdom. In a 1974 article entitled "Do Not Despair," he wrote "In general, the more food we eat in its natural state and the less it is refined without additives, the healthier it will be for us."[4]

---

[1] McKay, David O., Gospel Ideals, Improvement Era, 1953, p. 376.

[2] Quoted in Gerald E. Jones, *Concern for Animals as Manifest in Five American Churches...* Ph.D. diss., Brigham Young University (1972), p. 118.

[3] Joseph Fielding Smith, compl., *Teachings of the Prophet Joseph Smith*, Deseret Book Company (1977), p. 256.

[4] Benson, Ezra T., "Do Not Despair," *Ensign* 4:66 (1974).

In a talk he gave in 1979 to BYU students he said,

> To a significant degree, we are an overfed and undernourished nation digging an early grave with our teeth, and lacking the energy that could be ours because we overindulge in junk foods.... We need a generation of young people who, as Daniel, eat in a more healthy manner than to fare on the "kings meat"—and whose countenances show it. (Daniel I)[1]

In 1983 President Benson spoke to the students at Rick's College, and this talk was used as the First Presidency Message for September 1988. In it, he said,

> There is no question that the health of the body affects the spirit, or the Lord would never have revealed the Word of Wisdom.... Disease, fever and unexpected deaths are some of the consequences directly related to disobedience.... To a great extent, we are physically what we eat. Most of us are acquainted with some of the prohibitions of the Word of Wisdom, such as no tea, coffee, tobacco, or alcohol. But what need additional emphasis are the positive aspects—the need for vegetables, fruits, and grain, particularly wheat. We need a generation of people who eat in a healthier manner.[2]

President Benson's desire to repeat this message and to send it church-wide in the First Presidency Message through an official church publication should tell us the importance that he placed on it.

The pages that follow will present new nutritional facts that relate to poor health and premature death caused by bad food habits. Old fallacies about protein and some half-truths about fat will be discussed. The macho image of the meat eater will be examined. Data will show that cow's milk is not the perfect food for children or adults. Heart disease and its prevention will be explained in understandable terms. And most important, practical information will be given to help you make changes in your lifestyle and food habits.

---

[1] Benson, Ezra T., *Teaching of Ezra Taft Benson* (Salt Lake City, UT: Bookcraft, 1988), pp. 476-477.

[2] Benson, Ezra T., "In His Steps," *Ensign*, (September 1988), p. 5.

CHAPTER FIVE

FOOD AS FUEL FOR THE BODY
A PRIMER OF NUTRITION

A recent newspaper headline announced, "Vegetarianism Hits the Mainstream as Businesses Cash in on a New Diet." The article that followed tells how America is beginning to embrace a plant-centered diet. The "new" diet proclaimed by the newspaper account is exactly the same food plan prescribed by the Word of Wisdom over 160 years ago.

Until very recently, vegetarians have often been considered odd, ill-informed faddists; some people even thought vegetarian eating habits dangerous. Many vegetarians have endured hostility. There are many reasons for these attitudes, but one is that we feel threatened by any change in our long-standing habits. We tend to defend stubbornly what we believe and do.

Since the word vegetarian still inspires prejudice, I prefer the term plant-centered diet. In fact, a diet based solely on vegetables is not really a proper diet. D&C 89:14 makes that clear when it states that "*grain is the staff of life for man.*" We need a grain-centered diet based on cooked cereals, rice, pastas, potatoes, and bread, supplemented by cooked and raw fruits and vegetables. This diet is the Word of Wisdom food plan.

As a plant-centered diet has become more accepted, people have begun to cut back on the amount of meat they eat. In a recent issue of the *Journal of Food Products Marketing*, reporters wrote that "the most recognizable pattern in food consumption behavior in the last 20 years has been the shift away from animal products. American consumers are eating more crop products which include such items as cereal, sweeteners, fruits and vegetables." Approximately 10 million Americans now eat a plant-centered diet. Many world-class athletes in endurance contests (such as cycling, triathlons, marathons, and long-distance swimming) eat plant-centered diets and use "carboloading" to fuel their bodies. They eat primarily a complex-carbohydrate diet to store maximum amounts of glucose as glycogen in their livers and muscles.

The trend is obvious. *Vegetarian Times* boasts 200,000 subscribers. In one elegant Chicago restaurant, one in four patrons orders the eight-course, $55 "Vegetarian Menu Degustation."

At "The Source," a popular Hollywood restaurant, the veggieburger outsells the hamburger ten to one. Most restaurants now offer at least a few plant-centered dishes on their menus.

In some towns and cities, teenagers are taking the lead, reading books like John Robbins' *Diet for a New America* and echoing concern for the planet that is expressed in publications like *Worldwatch*. In that journal, researcher Alan Durning wrote, "American meat production overuses grain, water, land, fossil fuel, and electricity besides producing excess air and water pollution." Some of our children heard Tony White of the Earth-Save Foundation say,

> We graze cattle on the Western land, and the wolves and predators are killed so they don't kill cows. Then cows are killed and turned into hamburgers, and that kills people, and then the medical community kills research animals to figure out what killing us…. It's a cycle of death, you could say.

Let's look at some facts about man and animals. As a college student I was taught that man is omnivorous. And it is true that when famine brings unrelenting hunger, we have the ability to survive by eating animal products. However, we are healthier when we eats primarily a plant-centered diet.

Cholesterol is present only in animal food, which includes all egg, milk and meat products. Cholesterol is not present in plant food, and our bodies produces adequate cholesterol for our needs. We simply don't need to eat it.

However, we do have a limited capacity to process and utilize ingested cholesterol. The liver, which metabolizes cholesterol, is easily overwhelmed, and can handle only small amounts of it.

One of the first things I learned in medical school was the fact that rabbits, being herbivorous, rapidly develop atherosclerosis when force-fed food that contains cholesterol. Atherosclerosis is the same deadly narrowing of the arteries that we get when we eat foods containing fat and cholesterol.

There's another interesting fact about man and animals. Man and other herbivores have saliva that contains ptyalin, an enzyme that begins to break down complex carbohydrates into smaller nutritional components while food is still in the mouth and being chewed. Carnivores, on the other hand, tear up their meat in chunks and swallow it without chewing it. Their saliva doesn't contain ptyalin. They don't need it for meat contains no complex carbohydrate.

There are other differences between carnivores and herbivores. Carnivores have acidic saliva to help sterilize the contaminated meat that they must eat. Humans and other herbivores have alkaline saliva that helps digest food but does not protect against contamination. Humans and other herbivores have teeth for chewing; carnivores have fangs designed for ripping flesh, but no teeth for chewing.

Carnivores have twenty times the concentration of stomach acid as compared to humans and other herbivores. The acid is needed to sterilize food that is often grossly contaminated by bacterial infection. Humans, having comparatively little acid, may become very ill with contaminated animal products that would not harm a dog or a cat.

Humans and other herbivores have relatively long digestive tracts for the assimilation of necessary nutrients mixed with fiber. Carnivores have short digestive tracts, and eat animal food that has no fiber and is rapidly assimilated.

FUEL FOR THE BODY

As fuel for the body, food has seven important constituents: fats, carbohydrates, proteins, minerals, vitamins, fiber, and water.

FATS

Do we need fats in our diet? Yes. But unless you eat nothing at all, you can get all the fat you need in a plant-centered diet. In fact, most people eat far too much fat. The two essential fatty acids, linoleic acid and linolenic acid are never a problem except under the most unusual circumstances, e.g. prolonged starvation or fasting.

Nearly 50% of cow's milk calories are fat calories; this equally true of the products made from it. Eggs are 65% fat, mostly in the yolk. T-bone steak is 80% fat. Cheese is 50-70% fat; even 2% milk is really 38% fat.

Fat makes us fat. It makes us die prematurely from heart attack and strokes. Its relationship to the development of cancer is now well-documented. Cancers of the colon, liver, breast, ovary, uterus, bladder, prostate, and pancreas have all been shown to occur more frequently in people who consume a diet high in fats. An ongoing study by researchers at Cornell University is examining the diet in China. Led by Dr. T. Colin Campbell, the study shows that the average fat intake in China is 15 percent of total ingested calories; in some areas of China, fat comprises only 6 percent of total calories.[1] This compares with the average American intake of 40 percent. A similar study shows that Americans eat five time as much meat as the Chinese.

What's the result of the way the two populations eat? The risk of heart disease, cancer, diabetes, and osteoporosis is markedly reduced in the Chinese population, while these diseases are rampant in the United States.

After reviewing all recent scientific data, I believe that those presumed healthy should reduce their fat intake to less than 20 percent of total calories. If there is a known family history of heart disease, cancer, or diabetes, the fat intake should be less than 10 percent of total calories. This applies to both saturated and unsaturated fats. These recommendations are similar to those espoused by others. These recommendations also fit perfectly with the

---

[1] Campbell, T., *A Study on Diet, Nutrition and Disease in the People's Republic of China*, Division of Nutritional Sciences, (Ithaca, NY: Cornell University, 1990).

pronouncements in the food portion of the Word of Wisdom. They encourage the best possible health. They constitute a DISEASE PREVENTION diet.

The recommendation to reduce the fat intake to 10-20% of total food calories is not made lightly; I realize that it represents a substantial change in most people's eating habits. But I am convinced that there are great rewards.

How can you do it? With current labeling laws, it's very easy to monitor a 10 to 20 percent fat diet. First, all grains are less than 10 percent fat. All fruits and vegetables except avocados, olives, nuts, and chocolate are less than 10 percent fat. There is no need to calculate the fat content of grains, fruits, or vegetables, as long as you remember to eat few avocados, olives, nuts or chocolate. (This advice about avocados, olives and nuts is given despite a recent claim that these non-animal foods with high levels of fat may not be harmful and even could have a beneficial effect on lowering blood cholesterol levels. The true facts are not yet known.)

What about processed foods? The labels help you determine the percentage of calories that are fat. It's easy. You need only two numbers on the label: the number of calories in a serving, and the number of grams of fat in that serving. Since there are nine calories in a gram of fat, multiply the grams of fat by nine to know how many of the calories are derived from fat. Then compare the fat calories to total calories to get the fat percentage.

For example, if there are 100 calories and 2 grams of fat in a serving, multiply 2 grams by 9 calories. You'll find that 18 of the calories are derived from fat; 18 (fat calories) divided by 100 (total calories) equals 18 percent, the total fat content of the food.

That's all there is to it. You don't need food charts or a long list of "do's and don'ts." The best part is that a plant-centered diet provides all the vitamins, minerals, proteins, carbohydrates, and fiber you need. And there's no cholesterol to worry about, since plant foods don't contain cholesterol.

One caution: vegetable oils increase the body's ability to produce its own unwanted cholesterol. This concentrated form of fat also makes us fat. Leave it out of your Food Plan.

Cookies, cakes, pastries are notorious for their fat content. Candy made with milk chocolate also contains large amounts of fat. To know how much fat, look at the label. On a chocolate candy bar it will likely say "240 calories" and "14 grams fat." Do your calculating: 14 grams fat equals 14 x 9 calories or 126 fat calories. If the total calories are 240 and 126 of them are fat, then approximately 1/2 or 50% of the total calories are fat. That's too much!

CARBOHYDRATES

Before we ever heard the term "carboloading," we called complex carbohydrates "starches"; we were taught they caused obesity. Now we know that is not true; in fact, a diet composed mostly of complex carbohydrates coupled with a modest exercise program is the best way to lose weight. Complex carbohydrates should constitute the main part of a healthy eating plan—something that automatically happens when you eat a plant-centered diet.

The best carbohydrates are the complex carbohydrates found in plants, which have been the major part of man's food throughout recorded history. When boats arrived from Egypt laden with grain in the glory days of the Roman Empire, the people of Rome streamed down to the banks of the Mediterranean Sea for a celebration.[1]

Plant foods, consisting of complex carbohydrates, fiber, and some proteins, are slowly digested and delivered to the liver. Here the carbohydrates and protein are converted to glucose and amino acids, which are used by various body cells in their metabolism. Excess glucose is stored for future use as glycogen which is a complex carbohydrate available for energy. This process is the "carboloading" used by endurance athletes.

---

[1] The King James Version of the bible calls grain "corn" 107 times as an English translation. "Corn" is incorrect as the American Indians understand, for only they knew about corn in biblical times.

PROTEINS

Everyone knows that proteins are essential in food. But there are plenty of things about protein that many people don't know.

To begin with, most of us eat too much protein. It starts in infancy: human breast milk, designed by nature as the perfect food for newborns, contains only five percent protein; cow's milk and formulas based on cow's milk contain a whopping 21 percent protein of total calories. Human babies are slow growers compared to other species, and need much less protein for the growth of muscles and other tissues. As shown in the graph below, it takes 180 days for human babies to double their weight; after birth, rats double their weight in fewer than five days and their milk has nearly ten times the protein content than human milk.[1]

MILK REQUIREMENTS
TO DOUBLE BODY WEIGHT

	Protein Content GM per 100 ml.	Days Required to Double Weight
CARNIVORES		
RAT	11.8	<5
CAT	9.5	7
DOG	7.1	8
HERBIVORES		
GOAT	4.1	19
COW	3.3	47
HORSE	2.4	60
HUMAN	1.2	180

[1] Bell, G., *Textbook of Physiology and Chemistry*, 4th ed., (Baltimore, MD: Willams and Wilkins, 1959), pp. 167-170.

Another thing most people don't understand is that plant protein is just as good as animal protein. All vegetables, eaten singly or in combination, contain all the essential amino acids necessary for good health when caloric requirements are met. Because vegetables contain different amounts of minerals, vitamins, and fiber, it's important to eat a variety. But when you eat enough calories to satisfy your appetite, and the food consists of cereals, bread, fruits, vegetables, and legumes, you'll get plenty of high-quality protein.

There was a belief, long since refuted, that plant protein was inferior to animal protein. Unfortunately, it still persists as justification to eat animal products.[1]

When I was in medical school, we were taught about Kwashiorkor disease, a condition in Africa that was first attributed to protein deficiency.[2] It affects children and causes them to become emaciated with large, swollen abdomens. The physician who first identified the condition now declares that she had made a mistake: Kwashiorkor disease is caused by lack of calories, not a protein deficiency. As long as a diet is sufficient in calories derived from plant food such as grains, legumes, fruits, and vegetables, it will contain plenty of good protein.

CHOLESTEROL

We don't need an outside source of cholesterol—our body makes its own. The problem occurs when we eat too much: the liver has a limited capacity to metabolize the cholesterol we eat, and when the liver is overwhelmed, the excess cholesterol is deposited in places where it becomes harmful.

Where do we get cholesterol? Plant food contains no cholesterol. All animal products contain cholesterol; egg yolks have the highest concentration

---

[1] Pritikin, N., *The Pritikin Program for Diet & Exercise*, (New York, NY: Bantam Books, 1979); Remington, D., et al., *How to Lower Your Fat Thermostat*, (Vitality House International, 1983); McDougall, J., *The McDougall Plan*, (New Century Publishers,1983); *A Challenging Second Opinion*, (New Century Publishers, 1985); *The McDougall Program*, (New Century Publishers, 1990); Ornish, D., *Reversing Heart Disease*, (New York, NY: Random House, 1990).

[2] Williams, C., see McLaren, "A fresh look at protein-calorie malnutrition" *Lancet* 2:485 (1966).

(whopping 275 mg. per egg) of any food with the exception of liver. But who eats liver everyday? Chicken, fish, and red meat contain about the same concentration of cholesterol, so substituting chicken (even when the skin is removed) or fish for red meat is not a solution to the problem of eating too much cholesterol.

Meat and eggs are not the only culprits. Milk and dairy products contain it, too; even skim milk has 5 mg. cholesterol per serving and is limited by Dr. Dean Ornish in his regimen for reversing heart disease.

Dr. Jeremiah Stamler of Northwestern University and Dr. Richard Shekelle of the University of Texas studied 1,824 middle-aged Chicago men for a period of twenty-five years. They found a direct relationship between the increased ingestion of cholesterol and the increased risk of death from coronary heart disease. Dr. Stamler concluded that:

> Cholesterol-rich foods promote heart disease even in people with low blood cholesterol. And that's why eating less cholesterol must be of concern to all people, irrespective of their blood cholesterol level.[1]

FIBER

Fiber, the part of food that is not well absorbed into the body, is found in all plant foods and is totally absent in animal products. It's a new buzz word in the health magazines (not long ago it was called "cellulose").

Fiber serves a critical function in the body—and when it is removed from plant products that we eat or when we fail to follow a plant-centered diet plan, we suffer the consequences.

Fiber increases the water content in the stool, which eliminates constipation and reduces the risk of hemorrhoids, appendicitis, diverticulitis, and irritable bowel syndrome. Because food remains in the colon for a shorter period of time when you eat foods containing fiber, your colon is exposed to

---

[1] Stamler, J., "Dietary Cholesterol and Human Coronary Heart Disease," *Arch. Path. Lab.*,112:1032-1040.

fewer carcinogens, or cancer-causing agents. This may be one reason why the risk of colon cancer is lower among those who eat a high-fiber diet.

There's another benefit to fiber, too: soluble fibers form "gels" that delay the absorption of cholesterol. Some evidence also suggests that they increase the excretion of cholesterol in the bile, thus eliminating cholesterol from the body through the bowels. Wheat bran, an insoluble fiber, is inexpensive and easily available as a byproduct of white flour. Soluble fibers are found in oat bran, rice bran, pectin (in fruits), psyllium (the main ingredient in Metamucil™ and similar products), and guar gum (in beans).

VITAMINS AND MINERALS: LUBRICATION FOR THE HUMAN MACHINE

All of the vitamins and minerals that a healthy adult needs are readily available in plant food with the single exception of vitamin B12. Eating a variety of plant food easily supplies more than enough vitamins to meet the Recommended Daily Requirements (RDA) published by the National Research Council. These vitamins include beta-carotene (the precursor of vitamin A), thiamin (vitamin B1), riboflavin (vitamin B2), niacin, ascorbic acid (vitamin C), pyridoxine (vitamin B6), folic acid, biotin, pantothenic acid, cholecalciferol (vitamin D), vitamin E, and vitamin K.

Many of these essential vitamins are destroyed during the production of highly processed foods. Although foods are sometimes "enriched" by adding vitamins after processing, the closer we get to the unprocessed purity of the original plant food, the better chance we have of furnishing our bodies with proper amounts of vitamins.

THE EXCEPTION: VITAMIN B12

What about the exception? Vitamin B12, whose biologic name is cyanocobalamin, is an essential nutrient found in significant amounts only in animal products. But that doesn't justify eating large amounts of animal foods. You need only three micrograms of Vitamin B12 to meet RDA requirements (one microgram is one-millionth of a gram, and a gram is one fourth of a teaspoon). Furthermore, common bacteria in the intestine manufacture Vitamin B12, which is available for the body's use. Since we have the ability to store Vitamin B12, a typical adult may have a twenty-or thirty-year supply in his body.

Nevertheless, some medical authorities recommend a five mcg. supplement daily, especially for pregnant or nursing mothers.

What about megadoses of vitamins? Do they play a role in preventing disease? We don't know. Based on some theories, health magazines are beginning to extol them. In the health field, half-truths and misinformation create chronic anxiety and unanswerable questions like: "Am I doing the right thing? or "Am I doing enough?" Peace of mind is robbed. Chronic stress saps one's energy. We do not need to consider every theory that is on the cutting edge of research. Many of them will in time be proven wrong. How much better it is to be satisfied that you can trust in the Lord's word. One should always be suspicious of a new quick fix.

If you doubt the validity of nutritional information in this book, read the recommended books described in Chapter 13. All tell the same story and much of this information has been available for 25 years. The old aphorism "Be not the first the new to try, Be not the last, the old to cast aside" is worth your consideration.

The National Research Council has also established Recommended Daily Allowances (RDA) for minerals in food. These are minimum values, and are often not met by Americans who eat only highly processed foods. Since all the minerals that we ingest ultimately come from the soil, we can best obtain minerals from a variety of grains, fruits, and vegetables.

Calcium and iron are two important minerals that need special attention. Calcium is discussed in Chapter Ten because of its relation to osteoporosis. Iron is discussed later in this chapter.

SALT

The body has a remarkable ability to adjust to the excesses and deprivations in its environment. When too much salt is ingested, the kidneys excrete more of it to get rid of the excess salt. When too little salt is ingested, the kidneys excrete less of it to conserve the salt. This mechanism for balance is called "homeostasis," and variations of this principle are found in all organs of the body.

Hypertension, or high blood pressure, affects more than 40 million Americans and causes premature death from heart attacks, strokes, and kidney failure. The major cause of hypertension still is not known; Some less frequent causes are known and are treatable. Excess salt is not one of the causes of hypertension, but a plant-centered diet low in fat, cholesterol, and protein with *salt restriction* is effective in the control of hypertension.

IODINE

In the early part of the twentieth century enlarged thyroid glands ("goiters") were common in southern Idaho and northern Utah due to an iodine deficiency in the soil. Until iodized salt was introduced, many goiters were surgically removed. Iodized salt is an important constituent of food, especially in iodine deficient areas, and prevents the development of goiters.

IRON

A plant-centered diet provides plenty of iron for men, women, and growing children, although it is clear that menses in women causes blood loss and the need for more iron in food. The RDA for men is 10 mg, and 18 mg. for women. When body stores of iron are low, the body efficiently absorbs more iron to restore necessary supplies.

When the body has plenty of iron in storage, a message is sent to the intestine that reduces, but does not prevent further absorption. This mechanism can be overpowered by the ingestion of too much iron; the body has no method of eliminating stored or excess iron. There is also, regarding iron, a critical difference between plant foods and animal foods. Studies show clearly that 20 to 30 percent of the iron in beef, poultry, and seafood is absorbed by the body, compared to only 3 to 5 percent of the iron from vegetables and legumes.

One recent study suggests that too much iron can cause the development of premature heart disease. The resulting theory, based on a study of 2,000 Finnish men, suggests that meat—which leads to high absorption of iron—overloads the body with iron and leads to disease.[1] One health magazine writer already called iron, "the fallen angel of nutrition" even though this study is only on the cutting edge of recent research.

With recent challenges of the RDA and variations in recommended nutrients, how is it possible to balance nutritional supplements for proper doses? How can you make sure you're not getting toxic doses of certain vitamins and minerals that can't be eliminated by the body? The safest way is to prepare and eat a variety of foods low on the food chain—grains; namely, vegetables, legumes, potatoes, rice and fruits.

---

[1] Laffer, R., *Iron Balance* (New York, NY: St. Martin's Press, 1991).

CHAPTER SIX

CANCER

Cancer is probably one of the most dreaded words in the English language—and it describes an equally dreaded disease. As a physician I have watched helplessly during forty years of medical practice as patients and their families suffered its fatal progression. Our best modern surgical and medical treatments for cancer are only about 50 percent effective and the resulting trauma and financial burdens can leave permanent scars.

Despite all this, we can be incredibly casual and carefree when it comes to our personal habits. Last year I attended a medical conference in Wyoming with a group of LDS physicians and their spouses. The main topics of discussion were carcinogens in food, air pollution, and other environmental hazards—yet our first night's dinner featured a huge cut of roast beef, a dollop of blue cheese dressing on our salads, a rich slice of cheesecake for dessert, and plenty of milk and butter. The next afternoon, while sightseeing on a guided river excursion, we ate some of the blackest, burned baby beef ribs I have ever seen, even though that morning we had heard an excellent presentation about carcinogens in our food, including the hazards of barbecued food. Most of us have not faced the strong evidence that we can reduce our chances of dying from cancer by changing our eating habits. We know we can prevent lung cancer if we stop smoking, but many of us have not embraced the fact that a plant-centered food plan can largely prevent premature death from many cancers.

The statistics on diet-related cancers are sobering.[1] There are 155,000 new cases of colon and rectal cancer each year, and more than 60,000 of its victims die annually. Breast cancer has increased 24 percent in six years, and one out of every eight women alive today will develop breast cancer. Approximately 30,000 Americans die of prostate cancer each year, and 106,000 new cases are diagnosed. With our present diet, one out of every nine

---

[1] "Cancer Facts and Figures," American Cancer Society, (1990).

men will develop prostate cancer. Pancreatic cancer is the fifth leading cause of cancer death, claiming 25,000 Americans each year. These rates of disease and death will continue to increase until we change our eating habits.

Dr. Victor E. Archer, clinical professor in the University of Utah's Department of Family and Preventive Medicine, wrote in a 1988 nutritional report that

> Epidemiologic studies have indicated that between 30 percent and 60 percent of our fatal cancers are caused by "dietary factors." Extensive research on the nutritional components of the diet have yielded some positive findings in animals, but mostly indeterminate information in epidemiologic studies. *Diets that are low in fat, high in fibers, and high in fresh fruits and vegetables are recommended for CANCER PREVENTION* in spite of indeterminate human data, because of positive animal data or because this diet is beneficial for other reasons (such as preventing heart disease).[1] *(emphasis added)*

Archer's statement has since been bolstered by new knowledge and convincing epidemiological evidence.

LUNG CANCER

There is no need in this book to review the evidence that smoking is associated with a marked increase in cancer of the lung. But there is also evidence that lung cancer is increased by a high fat diet.[2] This association of high-fat diet and lung cancer is probably related to the immune system which is impaired by a high fat diet.[3] Vegetarians have twice the killer-cell activity of non-vegetarians.[4] This difference between vegetarians and non-vegetarians is not only due to the low content of fat in plant-centered diets, but could also be related to the presence of antioxidants (beta-carotene and vitamin C) in

---

[1] Archer, V., "Diet, Cooking Methods and Cancer," *Health Media of America*, vol. 6:12, (December 1988).

[2] Hinds, M., "Dietary Cholesterol and Lung Cancer Incidence in Hawaii." *Am. J. Clin. Nutr.*, 37:192-193, (1983); Jain, M., "Dietary Factors and the Risk of Lung Cancer," *Int. J. Cancer*, 45:287-293, (1990).

[3] Barone, J., "Dietary Fat and Natural-killer-cell Activity," *Am. J. Clin. Nutr.* 50:861-867, (1989).

[4] Barnard, N., "Foods and Immunity," *Guide to Healthy Living*, (July/August 1991), pp. 3-5, 15.

these foods. On the basis of recent and long-standing research both, lung cancer is a preventable disease. This we understand quite well.

BREAST CANCER

Equally true, but not as well known by American women, is the association of breast cancer and a high-fat diet.[1] (See graph below.)

MORTALITY RATE OF BREAST CANCER COMPARED TO FAT INTAKE

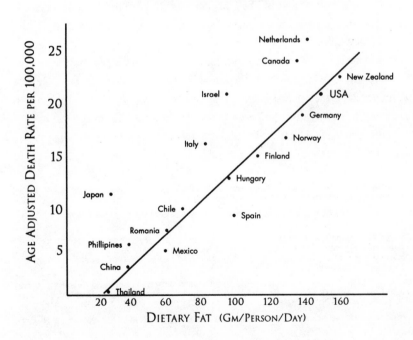

[1] Reddy, B., "Nutrition and Its Relationship to Cancer," *Advances Cancer Research*, 12:237-245, (1980).

Women know that the incidence of breast cancer is increasing; for they have heard the statistics that in 1960, one in twenty women would develop breast cancer in her lifetime. By 1990, one in ten women would develop breast cancer. It was one in nine in 1991, and recently it has been reported that, in 1993, one in eight women will develop breast cancer in her lifetime.[1]

Factors of physical exercise and hormone production (or ingestion) may be related to these statistics, but the preponderant evidence is that a high-fat diet is the culprit. Vegetarians have much lower levels of urinary estrogen than non-vegetarians. A high level of urinary estrogen is associated with a high incidence of breast cancer.[2] More estrogen is produced by eating a high-fat diet.[3] Since obesity is a result of a high-fat diet, obesity is associated with the high incidence of cancer.[4]

Women using birth control pills for more than eight years have twice the incidence of breast cancer, compared to non-users.[5] As Japanese women adopted a Westernized diet of 28% fat (compared to 8% previously) there has been a three-fold rise in breast cancer.[6] And they don't eat nearly as much fat as the 40% fat diet consumed by American women.

If one asks, "does changing to a plant-centered diet decrease the chance of developing breast cancer," the answer is "yes." Women in a Seattle experiment decreased their fat consumption from 40% to 20% and their breast cancer rate fell one-third compared to others who did not change their diet.[7] Most researchers feel that a diet of 10% fat will even be more effective in reducing the incidence of breast cancer.[8]

[1] Physicians Committee for Responsible Medicine (PCRM)—Cancer Brochure, PO Box 6322, Washington, DC, 20015.

[2] Kirschner, M., "The Role of Hormones in the Etiology of Human Breast Cancer," *Cancer*, 39:2716-2726, (1977).

[3] Schultz, T., "Nutrient Intake and Hormonal Status of Premenopausal Vegetarian Seventh-day Adventist and Premenopausal Nonvegetarians," *Nutr. Cancer*, 4:247-259, (1983); Bennett, F., "Diet and Sex-Hormone Concentrations: An Intervention Study for the Type of Fat Consumed," *Am. J. Clin. Nutr.*, 52:808-812, (1990).

[4] Gray, G., "Breast Cancer Incidence and Mortality Rates in Different Countries in Relation to Known Factors and Dietary Pracitices," *Br. J. Cancer*, 39:1-7, (1979); Hiryama, T., "Epidemiology of Breast Cancer with Special Reference to the Role of Diet," *Preven. Med.*, 7:173-195, (1978).

[5] United Kingdom Case-Control Study Group, "Oral Contraceptives Use and Breast Cancer Risk in Young Women," *Lancet*, I:973-982, (1989).

[6] Wynder, E., "Strategies Toward the Primary Prevention of Cancer," *Arch Surg.*, 125:163-169, (1990).

[7] Henderson, G., "Cancer Incidence in Seattle Women's Health Trial," *J. N. CI*, 83:336-340, (1991).

[8] Alabaster, O., *The Power of Prevention* (Georgetown, Washington, DC: Saville Books, 1991).

PROSTATE CANCER

Men are not exempt from a distinctive kind of cancer, for cancer of the prostate is likewise increasing rapidly. At the present time, one in nine men will develop cancer of the prostate. Of all cancers, only lung cancer kills more men than prostate cancer. Again, as with breast cancer, prostate cancer is linked to hormones, obesity and a high-fat diet. In this instance, testosterone, a male hormone is incriminated. Men, who consume more fat, are more prone to develop prostate cancer.[1] (See graph below.) A plant-centered diet reduces blood testosterone levels.[2] The non-obese male has a lower death rate than the obese from prostate cancer.[3]

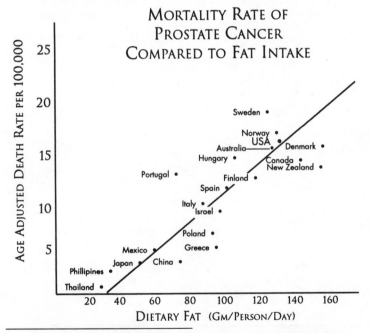

MORTALITY RATE OF PROSTATE CANCER COMPARED TO FAT INTAKE

---

[1] Armstrong, B., "Environmental Factors and Cancer Incidence and Mortality in Different Countries, with Special Reference to Dietary Practices," *Int. J. Cancer*, 15:617-631, (1975).

[2] Snowdon, D., "Diet, Obesity, and the Risk of Fatal Prostate Cancer," *Am. J. Epidemiol.*, 120:244-250, (1984); Hill, P., "Environmental Factors and Breast and Prostatic Cancer," *Cancer Research*, 41:3817-3818, (1981); Hill, P., "Plasma Hormones and Lipids in Men at Different Risk for Coronary Heart Disease," *Am. J. Nutr.*, 33:1010-1018, (1980).

[3] Mills, P., "Cohort Study of Diet, Lifestyle, and Prostate Cancer in Adventist Men," *Cancer* 64:598-604, (1989).

CANCER OF COLON-RECTUM

Next to lung cancer, the second most deadly cancerous disease in American is in the colon and rectum. It is rampant because of two dietary factors present in our American diet: inadequate fiber and excess fat. The relationship between dietary fat and death from colon cancer is shown in the graph below. The countries with a high-fiber plant-centered diet have the lowest death rates from colon cancer.[1] Numerous studies confirm the long standing declaration of Dr. Dennis Burkitt that low fiber in food is the offender.[2] Recent studies suggest that a high-fat diet and low fiber diet allow carcinogens to remain in longer contact with the bowel wall. Fecal bile acids and fecal cholesterol have been incriminated as co-carcinogens in these studies.

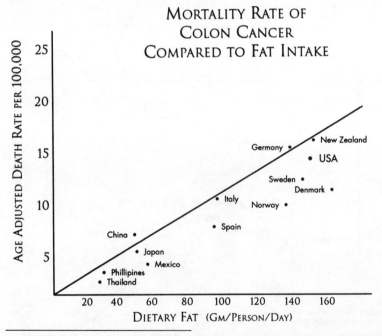

MORTALITY RATE OF
COLON CANCER
COMPARED TO FAT INTAKE

---

[1] Reddy, B., "Nutrition and Its Relationship to Cancer," *Advances Cancer Research*, 12:237-245, (1980).

[2] Burkitt, D., "Colon-Rectal Cancer: Fiber and Other Dietary Factors," *Am. J. Clin. Nutr.* 31:558-564, (1978); Freeman, H., "Dietary Fibre and Colonic Neoplasia," *Can. Med. Assoc.* 121:291-296, (1979).

Dr. Oliver Alabaster, director of the Institute for Disease Prevention at George Washington University, wrote in *The Power of Prevention* that,

> Environmental factors such as diet and smoking are now thought to cause as much as 90 percent of all human cancer in the United States, which means that cancer is potentially a *preventable disease.*[1]

Statistics show that smoking causes 30 percent of all deaths; therefore the way we eat is largely responsible for 60 percent of all deaths in the United States. Those statistics bear an important message: cancer is preventable.

Dr. Alabaster wrote further,

> The inability of a smoker to quit is as understandable as the inability of a compulsive eater to close a box of Swiss chocolate. Yet these forms of neurotic compulsion are not the reason we fail to make sensible adjustments in our diet. What we have always lacked is *informed guidance.* This situation has now changed. You can lessen your risk of cancer by planned changes in your diet.... A cancer prevention diet should become the normal diet for everyone.... We need not take into consideration every known food chemical and its possible interaction with other chemicals.... Every day there are women who endure the physical and psychological mutilation of a radical mastectomy (breast removal) for a cancer that may have been caused by excessive fat in the diet.[2] *(emphasis added)*

Where can we find the "informed guidance" to which Dr. Alabaster refers? We have had the answer for 160 years—the Word of Wisdom food plan.

Dr. John Bailar, former editor and chief of the *Journal of the National Cancer Institute*, editorialized in the *New England Journal of Medicine* that

> We are losing the war against cancer, notwithstanding progress against several uncommon forms of the disease, improvements in palliation, and extension of the productive years of life. A shift in research emphasis, from

---

[1] Alabaster, O., *The Power of Prevention* (Georgetown, Washington, DC: Saville Books, 1991), p. 13.

[2] Ibid.

research on treatment to research on prevention, seems necessary if substantial progress against cancer is to be forthcoming.[1]

EARLY CANCER DETECTION

Cancer begins with a single cell out of control. It takes years for its berserk reproduction to reach the size that enables detection. For example, a malignant breast lump would likely have been growing ten years to reach the size that would be noticed on self-breast examination.[2]

By the time the physician sees a smoker's cancer in an x-ray, it is almost invariably too late. The cancer has spread beyond control, through the blood stream and lymphatic systems. Palliation with chemotherapy, new drugs and radiation have not made a great difference in outcome. This is true about cancer of the breast, esophagus, stomach, gallbladder, liver, pancreas, prostate, ovary, kidney and lung.[3]

Much misery, suffering and expense can be avoided, if our efforts and health dollars are spent on prevention programs and education.

As President Ezra Taft Benson so clearly stated, "We need a generation of people who eat in a healthier manner."[4] We have the information we need in the Word of Wisdom—the rest is up to us.

---

[1] Bailar, J., "Progress Against Cancer?" *N. Eng. J. Med.*, 314:1226-1232, (1986).

[2] MacDonald, I., "The Natural History of Mammary Carcinoma," *Am. J. Surg.* 111:435, (1966); Gullino, P., "Natural History of Breast Cancer-Progression from Hyperplasia to Neoplasia as Predicted by Angiogenesis," *Cancer*, 39:2697, (1977).

[3] "Cancer Surveillance, Epidemiology and End Results Program, Cancer Patient Survival," Report No. 5, DHEW Publ. No. 77-992 *Nat. Inst. Health*, (1976).

[4] Benson, E., "In His Steps," *Ensign*, (September 1998), p. 5.

CHAPTER SEVEN

OBESITY

Despite spending $40 billion every year on weight loss schemes in the United States, we are bunch of fat people.[1] And it's not that we don't try: 30,000 of us each year have our jaws wired shut, and 100,000 of us each year are willing to mutilate ourselves with liposuction. Surgical tummy tucks and stomach stapling are common operations. Our diet soft drink consumption adds up to an average of 47 gallons per year for every man, woman and child in America.

Obesity begins in children because of their diet and the early formation of eating habits. Between 1963 and 1980 there was a 54 percent increase in obesity among children six to eleven years of age; there was a 100 percent increase in children classified as "super obese" (those who weigh twice their ideal weight).[2] In a 1987 survey, 63 percent of our teenage girls reported they were currently dieting on the day they were questioned; 16 percent of the teenage boys gave the same answer.

Recently, a father asked me to write a letter to authorize his two girls to substitute another drink to replace whole milk in their school lunches. This caring father had been reading the current nutritional facts about dairy products and realized a change was necessary. But it took a physician's letter to effect the change.

The parents of these children are obese, too. Some estimate that 40 percent of American women are overweight. And if you use "ideal weight" statistics which are lower than those established by insurance companies, then it is likely that 90 percent of women and 70 percent of men in this country are overweight.

---

[1] Obesity Update, (July/August 1991).

[2] Gortmaker, L., "Increasing Pediatric Obesity in the United States," *Am. J. Dis. Child* 141:535-540, (1987).

How did so many of us become obese? It's due to our love affair with high-fat foods, promoted by a clever public relations program sponsored by profit-minded industries. John Robbins' book, *May All Be Fed,* gives a lucid account of the manipulation over many years of our school education system by these industries.[1]

Let's look at school lunches. Unfortunately, 90 percent of the U.S. Department of Agriculture surplus food that is donated to the school lunch programs consist of eggs, high-fat cheese, butter, pork, beef, and whole milk. As a result, the average school lunch is over 40 percent fat. Skim milk and low-fat cheese are not available to children unless the school makes a special purchase.[2] By providing $3 to $4 billion a year in guaranteed supports to school lunch programs, the USDA is leading our children on a sure path to premature heart disease, cancer, adult-onset diabetes, and obesity!

How can we effect a change? It has to start with adults—and we need to start "cold turkey." I am aware that it is hard to face a period of cravings for certain foods, disruption of long standing habits and the doubt that change will even be successful. But, as a physician trying to help people rid themselves of tobacco addiction, I have learned that gradual elimination of bad habits does not work. When habits are well-established, it is too tough to change gradually. And, in some ways food habits are an addiction not too different from tobacco addiction.

The good news is that changing to a plant-centered diet brings some immediate and satisfying substitutes—a wide variety of delicious new foods. Also, in only a few days, a week or two at most, feelings of well-being and the assurance that you are doing the right thing take over. It has been my personal observation that, in contrast to the high failure rate in attempts to stop smoking, the success rate in changing to a healthier diet is excellent. If it is introduced properly, it becomes a permanent lifestyle. Beside that, a plant-centered diet helps the food budget; it saves on the cost of groceries.

As parents, you can teach by your example. Use patience and understanding as you introduce your children to the much-needed Word of Wisdom food plan based on grains, potatoes, rice, fruits, and vegetables. Let

---

[1] Robbins, J., *May All Be Fed* (New York, NY: William Morrow and Co., 1992).

[2] Bloyd-Peshkin, S., "What's Nutrition Got To Do With It?" *Vegetarian Times*, (September 1990), p. 52.

your children help with shopping as well as with the planning and preparation of meals. And provide plenty of positive reinforcement. Help them learn that righteousness is its own reward. They need to learn to do the right thing for the right reason. Fortunately, a slip or two in the learning phases are not catastrophes. The Physicians Committee for Responsible Medicine (PCRM) has a brilliantly colored poster for your wall or refrigerator door with pictures of luscious healthy foods in the New Four Food Groups. Write or phone them for one.

Physicians Committee for Responsible Medicine
P.O. Box 6322
Washington, DC
202/686-2210

Like the people in the Book of Daniel who ate a plant-centered diet, you'll start to feel better physically almost immediately, more than compensating for the foods you miss eating.

There's an even greater benefit: unlike all the other unsuccessful diets you've tried, this food plan lets you eat as much and as often as you want. The only caution is to limit both animal and vegetable fats and sweets; for sweets are loaded with empty calories and contain no fiber, vitamins, or minerals.

Most importantly, you'll lose weight—and you'll be protected from premature death due to cancer, strokes, and heart disease.

CHAPTER EIGHT

HEART DISEASE

I had always considered Nathan Pritikin as the pioneer of diet change to prevent heart disease. His first book was published in the late 1970s.

Recently I learned of Dr. Ray G. Cowley, an LDS doctor who preceded Pritikin with an article in the August 1969 *Improvement Era* entitled, "An 1833 Guide for the Prevention of Heart Disease." With remarkable clarity for those times he outlined a good diet program after these statements,

> There is the strong relationship between a high incidence of atherosclerosis and dietary change incident to improved economic status, such as the greater consumption of animal protein, saturated fat, refined carbohydrate and the decreased use of grains. Although this relationship is now supported by almost incontrovertible proof, the medical profession has been slow to accept findings that decimate a long standing and traditional dictum that a steady and large dietary intake of animal or fowl origin meat is essential to good health.[1]

He was referring to the 1833 Word of Wisdom revelation; with the medical evidence we have today, we can see that his statement, made nearly a quarter century ago, is correct. For the interested reader, the full text of Dr. Cowley's article from the August 1969 issue of the *Improvement Era* is reproduced in Appendix A of this book.

Doctors like to find obscure causes of heart disease. But even after sophisticated tests and laboratory studies, 99 times out of 100 we find ourselves face-to-face with the same problem: a bad heart devastated by clogged coronary arteries. We call it coronary heart disease, and it afflicts millions of Americans. It's the most common cause of death in this country. More than 1.5 million Americans have heart attacks every year—and for one-third of them, the heart attack is the first indication that something is wrong.[2]

---

[1] Cowley, R., "An 1883 Guide for the Prevention of Heart Disease," *Improvement Era*, (August 1969), pp. 60-63.

[2] "Heart and Stroke Facts," *American Heart Association*, (1991).

Coronary heart disease does not start with a heart attack. It's a gradual process that occurs over many years due to lack of physical exercise and a diet high in fat. The two coronary arteries and their branches, which supply the heart muscle, are gradually narrowed by cholesterol deposits and associated changes, a process that is called atherosclerosis. These narrowed arteries gradually carry less blood to the working heart muscle, which requires constant food and oxygen.

In addition to the gradual narrowing of the coronary arteries by cholesterol (atherosclerosis), these arteries can be temporarily narrowed by spasm. This, of course, also allows less blood to be transported to the heart muscle. Such a spasm can be triggered by a heavy meal, anger, or sudden excitement.

Temporary chest pain, called "angina," occurs when the heart muscle receives insufficient oxygen to carry out the immediate demands made upon it. The narrowed arteries or the added burden of spasm are the underlying cause. In a way, angina is a friend—it warns a person with coronary heart disease that there is something seriously wrong and they should stop the activity that exceeds the heart's capacity.

Unfortunately, angina doesn't occur until one or both of the coronary arteries are 70 to 80 percent closed off by atherosclerosis. Angina is not an early warning signal; it is a late signal, warning of serious heart disease and the possibility of a heart attack—a "coronary artery thrombosis" (a clot no larger than a grain of wheat that completely blocks the diseased artery). When this clot stops the blood flow to a part of the heart muscle, it immediately causes a "myocardial infarction" (the medical term for a heart attack, at which time part of the heart muscle dies).

A heart attack, then, is the tail end of abuse to one's heart that results from a long history of neglect. If the person lives, scar tissue eventually replaces the dead muscle.

What causes coronary heart disease? Experts agree that there are four major factors: genetic makeup, diabetes, hypertension (high blood pressure), and *a faulty lifestyle*. While you can't change your genetic makeup, you can make the lifestyle changes that will eliminate or markedly lessen the impact of the other three factors.

DIABETES

Diabetes is often associated with hypertension and premature heart disease. Why? Because this disease causes early atherosclerosis. Type I diabetes, which begins in youth, has a genetic origin, but a plant-centered food plan is very helpful in reducing the complications of atherosclerosis. Type II diabetes, which first occurs during maturity, can often be completely eliminated through a plant-centered food plan. (See Chapter Ten., "Maturity Diabetes" in this book.)

HYPERTENSION

Essential hypertension, the most common variety of high blood pressure, is an important cause of coronary heart disease. One in five adult Americans has hypertension; for some reason, it is much more prevalent and deadly among blacks. It is also five times more common among the obese, ages twenty to forty-four.[1]

While salt doesn't cause hypertension, salt restriction is helpful in its control. Even more beneficial is a plant-centered diet combined with exercise; the resulting weight loss generally helps control high blood pressure.[2]

LIFESTYLE CHANGES

Some medical investigators strongly believe that heart disease develops or worsens because of tension, anger, chronic stress, and the fast pace of today's life. The pursuit of material things and pleasure does tie us in knots. We are told that we do not take the time to smell the roses. Some physicians

---

[1] Lindahl, O., "A Vegan Regimen with Reduced Medication in the Treatment of Hypertension," *Br. Med. J.*, 52:11-20, (1984).

[2] Fries, E., "The Clinical Spectrum of Hypertension," *Arch. Int. Med.*, 133:982, (1974).

recommend relaxation exercises, yoga, and other forms of meditation; Dr. Dean Ornish devotes nearly a hundred pages to these ideas in his book *Reversing Heart Disease.*[1]

While this concept has some validity, there may be other lifestyle changes that are equally important. I see LDS Church members responding to the heavy demands of a rapidly growing church. Schedules are so busy that there is little time to relax. Stress seems extraordinary.

Many church members and non-members have learned that acts of service bring comfort and satisfaction to the giver. This knowledge sustains them. Peace of mind replaces anxiety and tension. These thoughtful acts of service may be more important than doctor's pills or relaxation exercises.

We do need peace of mind, absence of anxiety, a serenity with the awareness that we are making progress to eternal goals. We know the direction in which we want to go each day. Our relation to Deity is much improved when we sit down to read and ponder the scriptures, by gathering our children together for an evening to discuss family values, by organizing reunions for our extended families, by feeling the peace that comes with a visit to the temple of the Lord. The word recreation is a noun that implies taking action to enliven, to renew, perhaps to carry out the covenants we have made. Recreation could well mean to strive toward and recreate the relationship we once had with our Father in Heaven. These activities recharge our batteries much better than the world can with anything it has to offer.

Having material possessions that we use unwisely can harm us eternally. Smoldering anger or chronic resentment without the healing power of forgiveness can spiritually canker a lifetime and can cause coronary artery spasms.

Since our genes, our lifestyles, our eating habits, and our exercise patterns all intermingle to produce a certain level of health, especially the health of our hearts, we need to evaluate our health frequently. It's important to have periodic physical examinations with blood and urine tests. With these evaluations, physicians can detect early treatable disease and assess the progress of our disease prevention programs.

---

[1] Ornish, D., *Reversing Heart Disease* (New York, NY: Random House, 1990).

TESTS OF THE HUMAN HEART

Unfortunately, it's not easy to test the health of the human heart. A "normal" electrocardiogram (ECG) means little. Even a normal stress-treadmill ECG with exercise should not be reassuring. Why? Because one coronary artery or its branch must be more than 70 per cent closed before the test becomes positive. A person with 50 per cent obstruction of his or her coronary arteries would likely have a normal test. Also, false positive tests approach 30 per cent.

ULTRASOUND TESTS

Then what should be done to test the health of the circulatory system? In body areas other than the heart, modern ultrasound studies are able to define how much atherosclerosis exists in the arteries. For example, carotid artery studies (assessing the main arteries to the brain) are quite accurate with modern ultrasound techniques. This is also true in the leg arteries.

The ultrasound test, known as echocardiography, uses sound waves to assess heart valves, heart chamber size, heart wall thickness, heart flow dynamics, but it does not give much information about coronary artery blood flow. The large volume of blood in and around the heart precludes any accuracy with current ultrasound techniques.

Several other tests are available to assess the health of the heart.

1. ANGIOGRAPHY

To perform this definitive test, a physician threads a tube from an artery in an arm or leg to the heart area; a dye injected through the tube creates x-ray images of the coronary arteries. The test is expensive—generally between $5,000 and $6,000 and, because the procedure (catheterization) may disturb the heart rhythm, it carries a small risk of sudden death. A few medical centers have developed angiograms that feature digital measurements, eliminating some of the guesswork involved in visual estimations of coronary artery closure.

2. Thallium Stress Test

The imaging technique used in the Thallium Stress Test identifies impaired blood flow to the heart muscle. The test, which generally costs between $1,000 and $2,000, requires intravenous injection of radioactively-tagged thallium into a vein while the person is exercising.

A camera sensitive to gamma rays measures the radiation in the heart muscle by producing colored pictures of the heart. With exercise, poorly oxygenated heart muscle is differently colored than healthy heart muscle. With rest, the colors reverse—the poor heart muscle finally gets a portion of the thallium; the healthy heart muscle has been flushed of the thallium by its good blood supply.

Even the Thallium Stress Test has its drawbacks, though. It is inaccurate enough that one physician states that the test incorrectly identifies, as irreversibly damaged, nearly half the regions with only decreased blood supply.

3. Positron Emissions Tomography

Recently developed as a non-invasive diagnostic procedure, the positron emissions tomography appears to be accurate and sensitive, but is available in only a few medical centers. It cost around $1,500 and requires no cutting or radiation. It uses positron rays to create colored simulations of blood flow in the heart. During the test, the patient lies down comfortably, surrounded by this huge machine. As it becomes more available, researchers can determine its usefulness as a diagnostic tool in the fight against heart disease.

When an accurate, non-invasive and easily performed technique for studying coronary arteries is developed, it will cause a tremendous change in most everyone's behavior. For example, if you knew that you had a 30 per cent closure of a coronary artery (which would be symptomless) you would be able with today's knowledge to change your food and exercise habits and halt or even reverse the disease process. This test of the future will enable people to assess with accuracy the progress of their heart disease prevention programs. People will be able to prevent the heart disease which plagues our society today.

The idea of a prevention program, rather than a treatment program, is still desperately needed to promote better health. Maybe an abrasive slogan like "Why try to fix it, when one can prevent it" will jolt people hard enough to make them consider a change in lifestyle, especially a bad food habit.

Since no accurate, easily performed non-invasive tests are available, the only sensible alternative is to rely on the facts about fat and cholesterol. With those facts in mind, the best protection is a plant-centered food plan, such as the one prescribed by the Word of Wisdom. It is a wise program revealed by our Father in Heaven for our benefit. Those who follow such a food plan are given the following marvelous promise, from D&C 89:18-21:

> "And all saints who remember to keep and do these sayings, walking in obedience to the commandments, shall receive health in their navel and marrow to their bones;
> "And shall find wisdom and great treasures of knowledge, even hidden treasures;
> "And shall run and not be weary, and shall walk and not faint.
> "And I, the Lord, give unto them a promise, that the destroying angel shall pass by them, as the children of Israel, and not slay them. Amen."

CHAPTER NINE

OSTEOPOROSIS: OUR LOVE AFFAIR WITH MEAT, EGGS AND MILK

Osteoporosis is perhaps the most misunderstood and serious medical problem you're likely to face. It has nothing to do with cholesterol or fat. And it's not prevented by drinking plenty of milk. Its sinister presence lies in the realm of protein metabolism—and its prevention lies in a plant-centered diet.

For me, the end of a love affair with meat, eggs and milk began while reading the chapter on Osteoporosis in Harrison's 1977 edition of *Principles of Internal Medicine*. Harrison stated that,

> Another factor which some have implicated in bone loss is the possibility that excessive acid intake, particularly in the form of high-protein diets, results in "dissolution" of bone in an attempt to buffer the extra acid.[1]

We now know that Harrison's succinctly stated theory is true; it's been documented by 20 years of scientific medical evidence.[2]

Osteoporosis is the term used to describe a variety of diseases characterized by a reduction in the mass of bone to a level below that required for adequate mechanical support of the body.

Rarely, heredity disorders, an overactive thyroid, excess adrenal hormone, calcium and phosphorus disorders, and kidney disease can cause

---

[1] Harrison, *Principles of Internal Medicine*, 8th ed., vol. II, p. 2029.

[2] Licata, A., "Acute Effects of Dietary Protein on Calcium Metabolism in Patients with Osteoporosis," *J. Gerontol*, 36:14-19, (1982); Allen, L., "Protein Induced Hypercalciuria: A Long-term Study," *Am. J. Nutr.*, 32:741-749, (1979); Schuette, S., "Studies on the Mechanishm of Protein-induced Hypercalciuria in Older Men and Women," *J. Nutr.*, 110:305-315, (1980); Hegsted, M., "Long-term Effects of Protein Intake on Calium Metabolism in Young Adult Women," *J. Nutr.*, 111:244-251, (1981).

osteoporosis. Even caffeine, alcohol, smoking, and the phosphoric acids in soft drinks have some tendency to promote osteoporosis.

However, the common cause of this devastating disease is an improper diet and poor exercise.

Osteoporosis is common, widespread, debilitating, and expensive. It's estimated that more than 25 million Americans have osteoporosis, resulting in more than 1.3 million fractures each year, including 250,000 hip fractures. Half of all people with hip fractures require institutional care, and one in seven die shortly after the fracture from its complications. The annual cost of medical care associated with osteoporosis nationwide exceeds $10 billion.

The common form of osteoporosis is caused by the excessive loss of calcium. It is the result of long-standing ingestion of excess animal protein and lack of exercise.[1] Let me explain. Eating too much protein with its high amino acid content will load the body excessively with acids. The body, in order to maintain a critical level of acid-alkaline balance for thousands of orderly functions, must neutralize this excess acid, and does so by buffering (neutralizing) with calcium from the bones. But in this process, calcium is mobilized out of bone and excreted in the urine. It is a disease of calcium loss, not a calcium deficiency. As Harrison's book states, "There is no difference in the calcium intake of [the] osteoporotic compared with control subjects of similar age and sex."[2]

A plant-centered diet, with its high complex-carbohydrate content, its high fiber content, its minerals (adequate calcium) and vitamins and especially its *low but essential protein content* is necessary for the body and *is the preventative diet* against the misery of osteoporosis.

Lack of exercise is the other factor in the development of osteoporosis. This is best illustrated by noting what happens to bedridden people. They very rapidly lose calcium in their bones and are prone to bone fractures with any activity. The opposite is true: the more the bones in the arm, leg, or back are used, the stronger they become. Activity deposits calcium into bones.

---

[1] Koop, C., *The Surgeon General's Report on Nutrition and Health*, United States Department of Health and Human Services, (Rocklin, CA: Prima Publishing and Communications, 1988); Orwall, E., "The Rate of Bone-Mineral Loss in Normal Men and the Effects of Calcium and Cholecalciferol Supplementation," *Ann. Intern. Med.*, 112:29-34, (1990); Ris, B., "Does Calcium Supplementation Prevent Postmenopausal Bone Loss," *New Eng. J. Med.*, 316:173-177, (1987).

[2] Harrison, "Principle of Internal Medicine," 8th ed., vol. II, p. 2028.

In our society there are other obvious conditions that will make an individual more susceptible to osteoporosis. The alcoholic, who gets a large portion of his or her calories from alcohol and fails to take proper nourishment, will become osteoporotic. The smoker, whose appetite is diminished and who eats poorly, will be osteoporotic. A person who drinks three cups of coffee containing caffeine will, for the next several hours, triple his or her calcium losses in the urine. An elderly person, with a constrained budget or limited ability to prepare healthy food, will almost surely become osteoporotic. A teenager, overly focused about her slender figure and eating a poor diet, will lose bone calcium. The homeless almost surely will develop the disease because of their lifestyle and diet.

While this disease is widespread in our affluent Western Society osteoporosis is virtually nonexistent in billions of people in Africa and Asia where animal products are rarely eaten and milk products are virtually unknown. For example, the Chinese eat mainly rice, potatoes, beans, corn, wheat, barley, oats, fruit and vegetables. Their babies are breast fed and then weaned to this diet. The bones and teeth of children and adults are strong and healthy.

The average American eats 2-5 times as much protein as he or she needs. The daily protein intake of Americans is 90-120 grams and represents about 25% of total calories. The ideal protein intake is 20-40 grams per day, representing about 10% of total calories. The World Health Organization recommends 37 grams of protein per day and good scientific data shows that 20 grams will maintain positive nitrogen balance—a measure of adequate protein.[1]

We need to reduce our intake of protein. Knowing the cause of osteoporosis enables us to design a lifelong program of prevention centered on the truths taught in the Word of Wisdom food plan.

---

[1] Rose, W., "The Amino Acid Requirements of Adult Man," *Nutrition Abstracts and Review,* 27:631; McLaren, D. "The Great Protein Fiasco," *Lancet,* 2:93, (1974); Irwin M., "A Conspectur of Research on Protein Requirements of Man," *J. Nutr.,* 101:385, (1971); Abdulla, M., "Nutrient Intake and Health Status of Vegans," *Am. J. Cln. Nutr.,* 34:2464, (1981).

CHAPTER TEN

MATURITY DIABETES (ADULT-ONSET DIABETES OR TYPE II DIABETES)

Juvenile diabetes, called Type I diabetes or insulin dependent diabetes, has been present since antiquity. The Chinese described this condition nearly three thousand years ago. In 70 A.D., a Greek named Artaeus clearly described it; he coined the term diabetes from a Greek word meaning "to run through," because of the excess urine (polyuria) that is associated with the disease. Type I diabetes is genetic and is 20-50 times more frequent in persons who have parents or siblings with the disease. Today, Type I Diabetes results in devastating complications such as premature heart disease, blindness, end-stage kidney disease, strokes, amputations, neuropathy (diseased nerves) and impotence. It is present all over the world.

In Type I diabetes, the production of insulin in the pancreas gradually stops. Since insulin is needed by every body cell to utilize glucose for energy, the blood glucose level rises if insulin is deficient or absent. When insulin was discovered in the 1920's, researchers hoped that it would eradicate the disease. While insulin does not cure Type I Diabetes, insulin and a plant-centered diet does enable the insulin dependent to have a longer life and better lifestyle.

But we now have a new and much more common disease that has developed in the last half of the twentieth century. It is called "maturity diabetes," "adult onset diabetes" or "Type II diabetes." It occurs in any society that gives up a plant-centered diet and switches to a diet that is focused on animal food. It is almost unknown in Asian and African countries where plant-centered diets are the norm. Usually not insulin-dependent, it could well be named a disease of "fatness and indolence" since it is related to obesity and lack of exercise as well as a faulty diet.

Recent studies show that in contrast to Type I diabetics, where the pancreas does not produce enough insulin, Type II diabetics have normal or even super-normal insulin levels in the blood. But the cells of the body which need the insulin are in some way insensitive to it and they are unable to utilize the glucose for energy; the blood glucose remains high. Although the mechanism is not clear, this state of hyperglycemia (high blood sugar) leads to the same complications that exist with Type I diabetes.

There is no doubt that maturity diabetes is associated with high fat and low fiber in food. Studies reveal that the average American diet leads to high blood insulin, hypertrigliceridemia (high blood fat) and causes high blood sugar.[1] Placing patients with maturity diabetes on a low fat diet quickly lowers the blood sugar. Most patients with maturity diabetes are able to stop the use of insulin or markedly reduce the dose of insulin.[2]

It is estimated that 14 million Americans have this disease and approximately one half of them do not know they have it. One fourth of the patients requiring artificial kidney dialysis have diabetes. Every year, 150,000 people die prematurely of this disease and its complications. The annual cost is $20.4 billion and rising every year.[3]

UTAH: KUDOS AND CONCERNS

Utah, with its preponderant Mormon population has one of the best records of vital statistics that relate to deaths caused by smoking, alcohol or drug abuse.

Utah, however, has a higher death rate due to diabetes than the national average.[4] Utah's death rate due to diabetes has increased 60% from 1981 to

---

[1] Olefsky, J., "Reappraisal of the Role of Insulin in Hypertriglyceridemia," *Am. J. Med.*, 57:551-560, (1970).

[2] Kipnis, J., "Insulin Secretion in Normal and Diabeic Individuals," *Advances Int. Med.*, 161:103-135, (1970).

[3] "Diabetes Facts You Should Know," American Diabetes Assoc., (1990).

[4] Utah Dept. of Health, Bureau of Records, Chronic Disease Control, Salt Lake City, UT.

1991. Arizona, during the same period of time had an increase of 16% which is about the national average of 20%.[1] The statistics are not favorable for the nation and they are alarming for Utah. (See graph below.) Utah's increase in deaths related to diabetes is three times the national average. The statistics are mainly a reflection of poor eating habits.

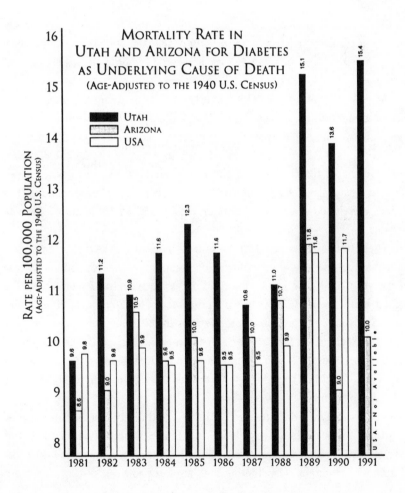

[1] Arizona Dept. of Health, Bureau of Records, Chronic Disease Control, Phoenix, AZ.

SOUTHWEST INDIANS: THEIR PROBLEM

In Arizona, where I practiced Nephrology, maturity diabetes and its complications have also become a serious affliction in the American Indian population.

Before the Indians began to eat white man's food, they ate foods consisting of beans, squash, corn, prickly pear (cactus) pods, mesquite bean flour, cholla cactus buds, seeds, oak acorn, and a little meat obtained by hunting.

After World War II, the U.S. government began giving the Indians U.S. surplus commodities, consisting of cheese, lard, butter, peanut butter and meat; this tax-supported generosity has created a nation of Indian diabetics.

The Indians began to eat a consistently high-fat diet with little complex carbohydrate or fiber; they also abandoned physical exercise. When these lifestyle changes were superimposed on a susceptible genetic makeup, the Indians developed a high incidence of obesity and an epidemic of Type II diabetes.

There are now over 250,000 Indian diabetics in Arizona and it is estimated that the annual cost of treating them will rise to two billion dollars by the year 2000. The Pima tribe residing in south central Arizona have the highest incidence of diabetes in the world. More than 50 percent of all adults over 35 years of age are diabetics. Diabetes in this population has increased over 40 percent in the last 20 years. One half of the Papago Indians who have had diabetes more than 10 years complain of impotence. Tribal chairman Josiah Moore said, "If we don't turn this around, as a nation, in 35-50 years, we're down the tubes."[1]

Why is maturity diabetes such a harmful and costly disease? Because of its effect on the blood vessels of the body. Diabetes accelerates the development of atherosclerosis, resulting in a 340 percent increase in the risk of a fatal heart attack. Considering both strokes and heart disease, the death

---

[1] *The Denver Post*, (June 21, 1992), p. 8A.

risk increases to 410 per cent in diabetics. Blindness occurs because of retinal vascular disease. Amputations of limbs occur because of vascular disease. Kidneys, which consist largely of blood vessels, are gradually destroyed and kidney failure is common. The Southwest American Indians, with their high rate of diabetes, are sixteen times more likely to be on kidney dialysis machines than are non-Indian Americans.

Today ten dialysis centers in Arizona and New Mexico are required to take care of the consequences of eating an improper diet by our Indian population. There were over 700 Indians in Arizona and New Mexico on chronic dialysis or transplant programs in 1990.[1] Two-thirds of those 702 Indian patients had end-stage renal disease due to diabetes. One dialysis center in Southern Arizona treats patients in four shifts around the clock.

THE MICRONESIANS IN NAURU: THEIR PROBLEM

A similar situation exists on the island of Nauru in the South Pacific. The natives have the second highest rate of diabetes in the world, with Type II diabetes afflicting 34% of the adult population. Prior to the 1940s, these islanders ate a plant-centered diet, and were very healthy and free of diabetes. When it was discovered that the islands were rich in phosphorus, islanders began exporting the mineral to developed countries who needed phosphorus for fertilizer. With their new wealth, they imported meat and animal products from New Zealand and Australia. As their eating habits changed, diabetes and its devastating consequences became epidemic.[2]

The answer to diabetes for both American Indians and the South Pacific Islanders is the same answer that applies to all of us: maturity diabetes can be prevented through the plant-centered diet prescribed by the Word of Wisdom food plan.

---

[1] Narva, A., "Research data on End Stage Renal Disease (ESRD) Among American Indians," *Indian Health Service Kidney Disease Program*, Albuquerque, NM (1990).

[2] Ringrose, H., "Nutrient Intakes in an Urbanized Micronesioan Population with a High Diabetes Prevalence," *Am. J. Clin. Nutr.*, 32:1334-1341, (1979).

A WORLDWIDE PROBLEM

The World Health Organization recently reported concern about the changing food patterns of poorer countries as they improve economic conditions and achieve financial stability. Past history, such as the experience of the Nauru natives in Micronesia and the plight of Southwest Indians, suggests that societies that have lived for centuries on a plant-centered diet will soon develop diabetes and other degenerative diseases when they adopt the eating habits of the Western World.

The concern of the World Health Organization has far reaching implications for the LDS Church's missionary efforts. In the affluent Western World, where a change in diet would be beneficial, the Word of Wisdom food plan should be extolled. In the poorer countries where people are still eating a plant-centered diet, this healthy diet should be encouraged and expanded by education and agricultural expertise.

Since the word *Mormon* means "more good,"[1] Mormons can practice and proclaim a healthy lifestyle that not only includes the abstinence of harmful substances, but also includes a food plan which is a beneficial program against degenerative diseases that cause premature death.

---

[1] Smith, Joseph, quoted in Joseph Fielding Smith's *Teachings of the Prophet Joseph Smith*, (Salt Lake City, UT: Deseret Book, 1976), pp. 299-301.

CHAPTER ELEVEN

FITNESS AND HEALTH: THE DIFFERENCE

Fitness and health are not the same. Do you need proof? Take a look at the sports world. Professional football players have great physical strength, tremendous coordination, and incredible stamina. The best of them pump iron year round to maintain their fitness. They have developed huge muscles for the battles in the trenches; wide receivers can jump like gazelles to catch the football. While they are still young they become coaches, coordinators, and assistants.

They are fit for football. But does that mean they're healthy? Not necessarily. For, despite their fitness, many have developed premature heart disease. Professional football coaches Dan Reeves and Mike Ditka are both former players with premature heart disease that has required angioplasty or bypass heart surgery. They and other athletes like them followed good exercise programs, but usually failed to follow the other part of a program designed for good health: a plant-centered food plan. It takes both a sound diet and regular exercise to maintain a healthy body.

A number of studies over the last decade have proved that hard, aerobic exercise is not necessary for optimum health. Before these studies were published, physicians and exercise physiologists claimed that the heart needed to be exercised regularly at 70 to 80 percent of its maximum heart rate— considered essential to maintain a healthy heart. Formulas and point systems were available so that men and women in various age groups knew what heart (pulse) rate, sustained for what period of time, gave maximum and safe conditioning of the heart.

We know that a healthy body requires both a proper diet and regular exercise. But let's face it: some of us don't like to exercise. What follows are a few facts that might help you start if you're now leading a dangerous and sedentary lifestyle:

First, a daily walk gives you most of what you need to maintain a healthy cardio-respiratory system, strong bones, and supple muscles. You need to add this mild exercise (or its equivalent) to a wholesome plant-centered diet.

Dr. Arthur S. Leon and his colleagues staged a Multiple Risk Factor Intervention Trial, in which they studied 12,138 middle-aged men divided into three groups based on their level of exercise. During seven years of follow-up, those who exercised moderately had one-third fewer deaths from all causes, including heart disease, than those who were sedentary. Moderate exercise was defined as walking, gardening, or repairing items at home for at least thirty minutes a day. The mortality rates of those with high levels of exercise were not significantly different from those with moderate levels of exercise.[1]

In a 1989 article in the *Journal of the American Medical Association*, Dr. Steven Blair and his colleagues at the Institute for Aerobic Research reported an eight-year study of 10,224 men and 3,120 women, all of whom were apparently healthy. On the basis of a stress-treadmill electrocardiogram (ECG), they were divided into five categories depending on their fitness. Category 1 was the least fit, and Category 5 was the most fit.

After eight years the death rates of the five groups were compared. The men and women with the lowest overall fitness had three times the death rate when compared with the most fit group. But the greatest difference was between categories 1 and 2—proving that even a little bit of exercise makes a great deal of difference.[2] (See graph next page.)

In other words, walking for thirty minutes a day (the activity level of group 2) reduced premature death almost as much as running thirty to forty miles a week (the activity level of group 5). Furthermore, the sedentary people in group 1 had higher death rates from all causes, including cancer and heart disease, when compared to the other four groups with better stress-treadmill tests.

The greatest effect of exercise requires only a modest commitment to exercise. If you enjoy biking, jogging, swimming, tennis, or some other

[1] Leon, A., "Leisure-time Physical Activity Levels and Risk of Coronary Heart Disease and Death," *JAMA*, 258:2388-2395, (1987).

[2] Blair, S., "Physical Fitness and All Causes of Mortality:," *JAMA*, 262:2395-2401, (1989).

activity, and you do it regularly, you'll have additional protection against premature death by creating larger coronary arteries and a network of collateral circulation in the heart.

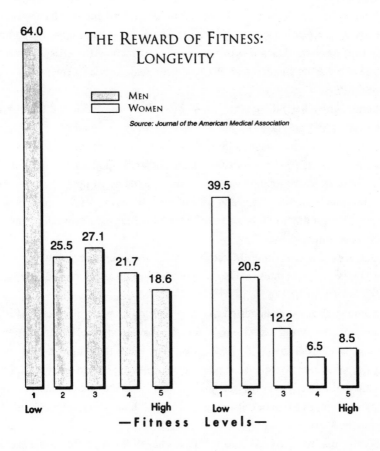

THE REWARD OF FITNESS: LONGEVITY

Nathan Pritikin, a photography genius who helped perfect the Norden bomb sight used in World War II deserves much credit for his pioneer book[1] advocating a plant-centered diet and exercise. Early in his life a diagnosis of serious heart disease was made on the basis of angina and electrocardiographic changes. With a change in lifestyle he lived many years, extolling with lecture and book the need for Americans to change their lifestyles. At his death due to lymphomatous cancer, his autopsy was reported in the *New England Journal of Medicine*. It documented the efficacy of the diet and exercise he championed: Pritikin's coronary arteries were completely free of disease.[2]

Some people believe that they are so busy they just cannot find time for a 30-minute walk each day. If you are one of them, you might consider a stationary exercise bike—something I've found to be an ideal way to get regular exercise. It's not dependent on the weather, air pollution, time of day, traffic, dogs, or your mood. If you add a music stand and a light source to the bike, you'll have an ideal place and time to read the scriptures or a good book. This physical program requires about 20 minutes four times a week for heart disease prevention.

But, first, get medical clearance from your doctor and start slowly. Learn about maximum heart rates (MHR) for your age group and pace your exercise to 70-80% of your MHR.

Some studies have suggested that people stay with exercise better if it's an enjoyable morning experience. Why? Most people feel better in the morning. It's harder to see the benefits of exercise at the end of a busy and tiring day. If a friend or spouse is equally committed, you can share a regular schedule and make it ever more enjoyable. But whether you exercise during the day or night, at home or outside, in a health club or swimming pool, go for it *regularly*. Make it a part of your life.

Again, one word of caution: if you decide to do more than walking as exercise, do it gradually, and get your doctor's approval. Always do warm-ups before strenuous exercise, cool-downs afterward, and regular stretching exercises to prevent injury to your muscles.

---

[1] Pritikin, N., *The Pritikin Program for Diet and Exercise*, (Bantam Books, 1979).

[2] Hubbard, J., "Nathan Pritikin's Heart," *New England Journal of Medicine*, 313:52, (1985).

CARBOLOADING

Carboloading, another buzz word of the 1990s, gives one food for thought, or more correctly, thought about food. Those who "carboload" may be the fittest and healthiest people in the world as they compete in contests of endurance and exercise.

What's involved? The technique consists of eating additional amounts of complex carbohydrates for several days before strenuous physical competition. These carbohydrates are processed into glucose and stored in the liver as glycogen, which is a complex carbohydrate of loosely bound glucose. The glucose is released into the bloodstream when more energy is required by hard-working muscle cells. In the jargon of the marathon runner, "hitting the wall" happens when all the stores of glycogen have been exhausted and each muscle cell is begging for more glucose for food and is suffering from lactic acid excess.

Non-athletes can increase their energy and capacity for work by doing what carboloaders do. Since there are no complex carbohydrates in animal products, it doesn't make sense to eat animal products for energy; grains, fruits, and vegetables are what provide complex carbohydrates. They, of course, come from a plant-centered diet.

An excellent example of the benefits of a plant-centered diet is Dave Scott, the greatest triathlete of all time. He has won Hawaii's Ironman Triathlon six times, three of them consecutively. This event requires three feats in succession: a 2.4-mile ocean swim, a 112-mile bike race, and, finally, a 26.2-mile marathon run.

According to Dave, a proclaimed vegetarian, "Animal products are not needed as food for people. They are unnecessary for athletes that are competing in endurance contests."[1]

Another long-time vegetarian, Sixto Linares, broke the world record in 1985 in a one-day triathlon contest. The event consists of swimming 4.8 miles, biking 185 miles, and running 52.4 miles.

---

[1] Personal telephone communication by author, (September 1992).

What these athletes have accomplished in competition has also held up in the laboratory. In 1968 a group of men exhausted themselves in a standardized exercise on stationary bicycles while being tested under three types of diets. The diets were (1) a high-meat diet, (2) a diet consisting of both meats and vegetables, and (3) a strictly vegetarian diet consisting of grains, fruits, and vegetables.

Those on the high-meat diet experienced exhaustion and muscle failure after 57 minutes. Those on the meat and vegetable diet bicycled for 114 minutes before becoming exhausted. But those on the vegetarian diet lasted 167 minutes—virtually three times as long as those on a high-meat diet.[1]

In essence, we are learning through scientific study that the truths found in the Word of Wisdom are just that—truths that stand up to scientific scrutiny. The "Church News" section of the *Deseret New* reported an address by Brigham Young University professor of geophysics and geology Alvin K. Benson, who said,

> Although Joseph Smith's calling was spiritual, God taught him both religious and scientific principles. The scientific principles include the law of health known as the Word of Wisdom... *It's exciting to see how continuing discoveries verify the wisdom and insight revealed to the Prophet in the Word of Wisdom, a revelation given when knowledge of nutrition was essentially non-existent.*[2] *(emphasis added)*

[1] Astrand, P., *Nutrition Today*, 3:2, 9-11, (1968).
[2] Benson, A., *Deseret News* "Church News" Section, (February 29, 1992).

CHAPTER TWELVE

BARRIERS AND PATHS TOWARD CHANGE

With all the information that is available, why is it so hard to change one's lifestyle, especially one's food habits? There are many reasons and you may recognize one or more of them that shape your attitude toward change.

WE DEFEND WHAT WE DO

Whatever our actions are, we think, consciously or subconsciously, that they are right (otherwise we would not do them). Even when we know at some point that our actions are wrong, we continue to defend that action and even look for further reasons to defend ourselves and our action. It is hard to admit we are wrong. It is hard to admit we need to change.

If we choose not to change, having good and sufficient understanding that change is needed, there can be no progress or improvement in our behavior.

WE WANT A QUICK FIX

Our society has come to expect instant gratification. We buy things with plastic money before we have earned the money to pay for them. To fulfill our dreams or desires, we can fly to other continents in a few hours. We expect an instant cure for medical problems—and have an arsenal of pills to help us sleep, lose weight and conquer depression.

Doctors have little to offer alcoholics and smokers for they all want a quick and painless fix. There is a "quick" and permanent fix in these conditions, but the sufferers have to do it by themselves.

There is no quick fix to prevent the degenerative diseases outlined in this book; the solution requires a change in lifestyle, a long-term plan of prevention. This plan was given to us over 160 years ago in the Word of Wisdom and, like all gospel principles, it requires personal change.

The Word of Wisdom establishes prevention as the key to good health and this has been emphasized over and over in these discussions. Medical treatment becomes necessary when we fail to follow a prevention program. What doctors do best is diagnose and treat "after" an individual fails in his or her prevention program.

For example, I was trained in medical school never to moralize or pass judgment on someone's conduct. When a young woman came to me with acute gonorrhea due to promiscuous sexual activity, I was expected not to lecture her about the danger of her actions that could cause permanent sterility or a serious, potentially fatal septicemia (blood stream infection). I was taught to make a proper diagnosis and give the best treatment, but not try to moralize. Yet, in my opinion, the best good for her was to tell her about the reasons and need for prevention. This might have helped to change her behavior. She needed a prevention program called abstinence.

WE BEHAVE ACCORDING TO OUR HABITS

The cliché that humans are creature of habit is true. In medical school I learned about the marvelous design of the brain with its intricate structure and organization. Our brains are programmed to respond to repeated messages along the same nerves, allowing us to play the piano, to remember names and phone numbers, to learn foreign languages, to operate complicated machines, etc. The brain loves repetition and routine. Decisions become almost automatic when we develop a habit. When we change those habits, new programs are needed to establish new automatic messages in the brain and it takes some time to develop a new habit. When a long-standing food habit is being changed, the new decision needs to be repetitively reinforced until it becomes a habit. The brain does love quiet routine and repetition. But in some ways those tendencies are a barrier to change.

What, then is the good news? For one thing, changing a food habit is much less difficult than ridding oneself of a tobacco or alcohol habit. It is not a true addiction, although you might think so for a few days. Newness, unfamiliarity and uncertainty are initial threats, but since there is no chemical dependency, within a few days you feel so much livelier and better that it compensates for the missing foods.

WE ARE MISLED BY THE POLITICS OF NUTRITION

Since everyone wants good health, everyone is looking for the right answers. Unfortunately, people are tugged and pushed in different directions by powerful forces that try to control their health habits. These are the "vested interests," a term sometimes replaced during the Watergate scandal with the term, "follow the money."

Where does all our money go? Presently we are spending 14% of our Gross National Product (GNP) for health care. Remember, this means trillions of dollars. The expense is growing by 10% each year and is expected to reach 20% of the GNP by the year 2000 unless there are some changes. Much of this problem can be traced to Washington DC where "big" government has become "huge" government. The politics of nutrition begins with policy-making agencies that have overlapping responsibilities. The National Institutes of Health, the U.S. Department of Health and Human Services, the National Research Council, the National Cancer Institute, the Office of the Surgeon General and the U.S. Department of Agriculture all need consensus opinions before making any recommendations to the lawmakers in U.S. Congress. Self-serving food industries, drug companies, medical associations, insurance companies and foundations have lobbyists who are paid to influence incumbent congressmen to support the views of the "vested interest" groups.

Many nutritionists say that government guidelines do more harm than good, for they represent a watered-down version of the nutritional facts. They are the result of "good ol' boy" policies in Washington where the guideline writers bow to the vested interests.

New government guidelines are always a consensus process where somebody produces a initial draft, other people hack at it and then all parties do some political horse trading. Guideline writers are hounded by industry lobbyists who submit written suggestions and then insist on subtle changes in guideline language that favors their products.

The U.S. Department of Agriculture has been caught up in this process for years. It has two opposing missions: one, to promote public health through a safe and beneficial food supply; the other, to promote U.S. agriculture, including meat, milk and eggs. It is impossible for the agency to encourage the marketing of these products and at the same time advise consumers to stop using them when they are found to be harmful.

The explosive incidence of diabetes in Indians can be laid at the door of the flawed policies of the USDA in its price support and subsidy programs. The U.S. taxpayer pays the meat and dairy industries to grow products which are not needed and the surplus is given to the Indians. In a sense, it is the taxpayers who are at fault for allowing this scenario. We provide the money.

Let's look at a 1990 publication, "Dietary Guidelines for America." It was produced by the USDA and the U.S. Department of Health and Human Services. This 28-page pamphlet begins with the sweetness of consensus: "These guidelines call for moderation. How, you might ask? Eat a variety of foods. Maintain healthy weight. Choose a diet low in fat, saturated fat and cholesterol. Choose a diet with plenty of vegetables, fruits and grain products. Use sugar only in moderation. Use salt and sodium only in moderation. If you drink alcoholic beverages, do so in moderation."[1] Does it sound sensible?

No, it is not, for on page 16, we read that the total fat intake should be "30 per cent or less of calories." This weak statement does not reflect the light of recent medical studies. In fact, this phrase "30 percent or less" is harmful

---

[1] "Dietary Guidelines for America," U.S. Department of Agriculture and U.S. Department of Health and Human Services, (1990).

because it blurs the resolve to change one's food habits. Reducing fat from the 37-40% fat presently eaten each day to 30% will not make a difference.[1] Furthermore, "or less" is a confusing term, lacking definition for the reader.

Dr. John Scharfenberg, a professor of nutrition at Loma Linda University and former clinician at the National Institutes of Health, says the USDA's dietary advice has always been a source of misinformation, much of it generated by or in support of the meat and dairy industries. This misinformation, Scharfenberg says, has "increased heart attack rates and cancer rates."[2]

FOOD LABELING LAW OF 1994

The food industry has been notorious for mislabeling their products. Using half-truths such as "lite" to mean variations in color, density, appearance and concentration, the food industry has confused the consumer. Percentages of fat in food have been deceptively tied to dry weight, rather than total weight including water content and calories.

For the past decade, the U.S. Department of Agriculture and the Federal Drug Administration have been working in committees to improve the food labeling laws because of the currently misleading information in them. During these years, the food industries, having a variety of vested interests, have watched and pressured for every advantage. Since a consensus was never ever really possible among all interested parties, late in 1992 President Bush stepped in and refereed the Labeling Law's final form. Defined in over 4,000 pages, it is effective May, 1994.

The new food label will look as shown below. I think you will find it very confusing.

---

[1] Browner, W., et al., "What If America Ate Less Fat?" *JAMA* 265:3285-3291, (1991).

[2] Scharfenberg, J., *Problems With Meat*, Woodbridge Press, (1982).

Nutrition Facts

❶ Serving size 1/2 cup (114g)
Servings per container 4

Calories 260   ❷ Calories from fat 120

❸

Amount per serving   %Daily value*

Total Fat 13g	20%
Saturated fat 5g	25%
❹ Cholesterol 30mg	10%
Sodium 660mg	28%
Total Carbohydrate 31g	11%
Sugars 5g	
Dietary fiber 0g	0%
Protein 5g	

Vitamin A 4% • Vitamin C 2%
Calcium 15% • Iron 4%

*Percents (%) of a Daily Value are based on a 2,000 calorie diet. Your Daily Values may vary higher or lower depending on your calorie needs:

Nutrient		2,000 ❺ Calories	2,500 Calories
Total fat	less than	65g	80g
Sat. fat	less than	20g	25g
Cholesterol	less than	300mg	300mg
Sodium	less than	2400mg	2400mg
Total Carbohydrate		300g	375g
Fiber		25g	30g

❻ 1g fat=9 calories
1g carbohydrates=4 calories
1g protein=4 calories

Fortunately, the first few lines are understandable, describing the serving size, total calories and calories from fat. This information is helpful, for one can know the percentage of fat in the food by a simple calculation. Knowing the percentage of fat in the food is an important fact. For instance, in the depicted food label, the fat content is 120 calories in 260 total calories of food as shown at the top of the label. This food therefore contains 46% fat (120 divided by 260 x 100). The rest of the label with two large sections is a math major's nightmare. The next section of the label says the fat is 20%. Do you know why? It will take you some time to figure it out. Suffice it to say, the rest of the data in the label about fat is based on the premise that a 30% fat diet is healthy ("recommended") with 65 grams of fat in a 2000 calorie diet. This is a premise that the label does not make clear. Furthermore, a 30% fat diet with 65 grams of fat does not fit with new nutritional facts.

The label compounds confusion in its last section of the label by using the term, "fat...less than 65 grams." What does that mean? Confusing? To me, this new labeling law confirms the statement made over 160 years ago that "In consequence of the evils and design which do and will exist in the hearts of conspiring men in the last day, I have warned you, by giving unto you this word of wisdom." (D&C 89:4)

The Medico-Pharmacologic Complex

This phrase was first used by Dr. C. Everett Koop after he left the Surgeon General's office a few years ago. He likened the term to President Ike Eisenhower's term, "military-industrial complex." He implied that a powerful combination of medical forces including physicians, related medical science researchers, drug companies and government agencies control the health care dollars in the country.

I should like to use this term in the same way and point out that our efforts in the health care have shifted away from the area of prevention in the last few decades. It is now focused primarily on treatment and illusive cures.

This is a major part of the mounting cost of health care in the United States and one of the causes of our deficit spending. And we are running out of money.

In the search for cures and treatment of disease, the United States is spending more and more money on new drugs, new detection methods and new therapies for disease. We have forgotten what was successful in the past and what could succeed in the future. We have neglected the science and promotion of disease prevention.

A large number of our children are unprotected from preventable infections because we have not required or implemented immunization programs. There is a question about the value of mammography in women under age 50.[1] Dr. Charles Smart, a well known researcher in this field, documents that recent improvements in mammography with two views and more frequent testing improves the success rate of mammography.[2]

One of eight American women living today will develop breast cancer and this statistic is worsening each year.[3] Mammograms will not change that statistic. What can women do about this? Women can change their diets.

Recent data show that medications are more expensive in the U.S. than in any place in the world. Pharmaceutical companies are responding to our desire for new therapies. We want the easy quick fix and they have found it very profitable.

We spend billions of dollars for heart bypass surgery and angioplasty while we neglect prevention programs that could eliminate these expensive procedures. The question could again be asked, "Why fix it when it can be prevented?"

Our government has fostered this medico-pharmacologic complex and we have allowed it, partly by apathy and partly by ignorance. If health costs are to be reduced, the government will have to rechannel taxpayer dollars to encourage disease prevention programs. Our congressional delegates and other governmental officials are currently struggling to solve the present

[1] Miller A., et al., "Canadian National Breast Screening Study: 1 and 2," *Canadian Medical Assoc. J.* 10:1459-1488, (1992).

[2] Smart, C., "The Role of Mammography in the Prevention of Mortality from Breast Cancer," *Cancer Prevention* (Philadelphia, PA: Lippincott, 1990) pp. 1-16.

[3] PCRM—Cancer Brochure, PO Box 6322, Washington, DC, 20015, (1992).

health care crisis with its burdensome cost and lack of medical coverage for many Americans. The only answer to the dilemma is to support a disease prevention program.

MISINFORMATION, HYPE AND HALF-TRUTHS

Most Americans are greatly interested in improving personal health. Nearly everybody has heard the new buzz words: "high-fiber," "low fat," and "low cholesterol." But good, solid information that can help change a lifestyle is hard to come by. We are confused because truth is mixed with misinformation, hype and half-truths. The news media, health magazines, health food stores and the food faddist next door bombard and confuse. If you ask what is the best way to separate truth from deception, the answer is, it is not easy to find one. I have tried to give you truthful information in this book. The books described in Chapter 13 are helpful in increasing your knowledge about the "new" facts of nutrition.

Some say that people are not willing to change their lifestyles in order to prevent disease and premature death. I don't believe this. I believe that when the truth about good nutrition is readily available and uncluttered by misinformation, there will be a great change in the lifestyles of many people.

In October 1992, the American Dietetic Association clearly reaffirmed its position paper on vegetarianism which appears as Appendix B in this book. It states that;

> A low fat, meatless diet reduces the risk of obesity, coronary heart disease, high blood pressure, diabetes mellitus, osteoporosis, diverticular disease, kidney stones, gall stones, and cancer of the colon, breast and lung.[1]

---

[1] "Position of The American Dietetic Association: Vegetarian Diets," American Dietetic Association Report, pp. 351-355, (1988); (reaffirmed October 1992).

Truth needs to be taught even when there is poor compliance. In October 1991, the nutritional researcher Dr. T. Colin Campbell addressed a prestigious medical research group, saying

> Why must we be reticent about recommending a diet which we know is safe and healthy? We, as scientists, can no longer take the attitude that the pubic cannot benefit from information they are not ready for. We must have the integrity to tell them the truth and let them decide what to do with it. We cannot force them to follow the guidelines we recommend, but we can give them these guidelines and let them decide.... We must tell them that a diet of roots, stems, seeds, flowers, fruits and leaves is the healthiest diet, and the only diet we can promote, endorse and recommend.[1]

He was speaking about grains, rice, potatoes, fruits and vegetables—i.e., about a plant-centered diet.

If tax money is rechannelled into education programs about prevention, it will have a positive effect on our nation's lifestyle. Overweight children need good education programs in their schools. The elderly need exercise programs and a proper diet to prevent osteoporosis. All of us need to be brought up-to-date about research that focuses on prevention rather than on treatments and cures.

[1] Campbell, T., quoted in May All Be Fed by John Robbins (New York, NY: William Morrow and Co., 1992).

CHAPTER THIRTEEN

THE BEST DIETS ARE ALL ALIKE

Scattered among the numerous diets that consistently fail are several medically-sound diets that follow the tenets of the Word of Wisdom. Only minor differences exist between these diets and the 160-year old guide.

These diets are plant-centered, with emphasis on complex carbohydrates, limits on protein, and severe limits on fat. In these diets, crop products (made from grains, rice, potatoes, legumes, fruits and vegetables) are the main source of calories.

The diets are also high in fiber and low in cholesterol. Flesh products (meat, fish, eggs and milk) are eliminated or strictly limited because of the reasons presented in this book. All of these diets require some physical exercise for maximum health benefits.

A comparison of these diets is shown on the following pages.

THE PRITIKIN DIET
BY NATHAN PRITIKIN

Published nearly fifteen years ago, this diet is a plant-centered diet, recommending no animal products except skim milk and a little meat. Eggs are excluded as are all dairy products except for the skim milk. Meat is limited to one-fourth pound of meat or fish daily. In *The Pritikin Program for Diet & Exercise*, the author states that "If you can do with animal protein only three times a week, so much the better. Ideally, meat and fish become condiments to flavor other dishes, rather than main courses." In addition to the diet plan, Pritikin stresses physical exercise.[1]

THE FAT THERMOSTAT NO-DIET DIET
BY DENNIS REMINGTON, M.D., GARTH FISHER, M.D., AND EDWARD PARENT, PH.D.

This sound weight control plan is based on a plausible "fat thermostat" theory well documented in today's medical literature. The program is a plant-centered diet combined with physical exercise. Spelled out in Remington's *How to Lower Your Fat Thermostat: The No-Diet Reprogramming Plan for Lifelong Weight Control*[2] this food plan allows "no more than three and one-half ounces to four ounces of meat daily" and a little skim milk. No other animal products, including milk and eggs, are recommended.

[1] Pritikin, N., *The Pritikin Program for Diet & Exercise* (New York, NY: Bantam Books, 1979).

[2] Remington, D., et al., *How to Lower Your Fat Thermostat* (Vitality House International, 1983).

THE MCDOUGALL PLAN
BY JOHN MCDOUGALL, M.D., AND MARY A. MCDOUGALL

Three books written by these authors have been published in the last 10 years.[1] *A Challenging Second Opinion* is an excellent book to clarify the need to change one's food and exercise habits. The three books present strong evidence that the best possible health is obtained by eliminating all meat, egg and milk products.

THE "REVERSING HEART DISEASE" PLAN
BY DEAN ORNISH, M.D.

This plan, in Ornish's book, *Reversing Heart Disease,*[2] documents the efficacy of a diet that not only prevents the development of coronary heart disease, but also can reverse it. With a content of 10% fat, this "reversal diet" is recommended for all who have proven heart disease or family histories of heart disease. Those without histories of heart disease and with cholesterol levels above 150 are prescribed a "prevention" diet that is 20 per cent fat. If the cholesterol level remains over 150 with the 20 per cent fat diet, he recommends the "reversal diet" of 10% fat. This diet allows no meat, egg or milk products except one glass of skim milk daily.

---

[1] McDougall, J., *The McDougall Plan* (New Century Publishers,1983); *A Challenging Second Opinion* (New Century Publishers, 1985); *The McDougall Program* (New Century Publishers, 1990).

[2] Ornish, D., *Reversing Heart Disease* (New York, NY: Random House, 1990).

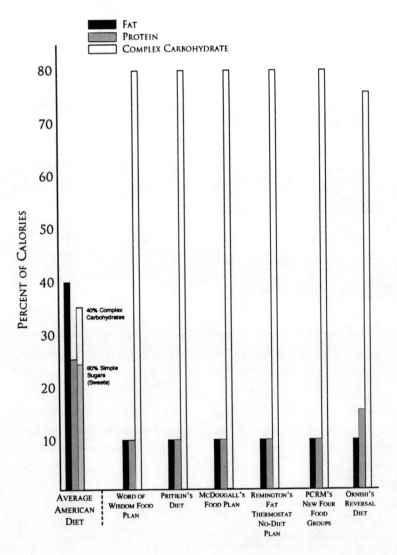

THE BEST DIETS ARE ALL ALIKE
(COMPARE WITH AVERAGE AMERICAN DIET)

THE FOOD GUIDE PYRAMID
BY THE U.S. DEPARTMENT OF AGRICULTURE

This food guide took nearly a decade to develop. After spending several million dollars, the department announced the Food Guide Pyramid in 1991. The "four basic food groups" (meat, milk, fruits and vegetables) were not changed, but were depicted differently, using a pyramid graphic (instead of a pie-shaped graphic) and including new recommendations for daily servings of each food group. The nutritional experts applauded this modest change, for the pyramid had been studied by thirty government and nutritional experts for three years after its initial development and had been approved by a joint committee of the U.S. Departments of Agriculture and Health and Human Services. It was a product of consensus.

However, lobbyists for the vested interests in the food industry pounced on Agriculture Secretary Edward Madigan and by complaining loudly, pressured him until he announced an indefinite delay for more study.

The food guide pyramid finally appeared in 1992 with only minor changes; this time Secretary Madigan withstood the pressure of the vested interest groups.

This Food Guide Pyramid, shown on the following page, is to be promoted in the schools and will be of some help. However, John Robbins has made this comment about this somewhat watered-down guide,

> The sadness is that this is still only a small step forward. Our children will still be taught, as truth, erroneous beliefs; beliefs that have been so relentlessly repeated that they continue to influence even those of us who know them to be awry. Our children will still be told to eat two to three servings from the meat group and two to three servings from the milk group every day.[1]

Unfortunately, this "Food Guide Pyramid" offers only broad guidelines; it will be manipulated by vested interests who tend to overpower the

---

[1] Robbins, J., *May All Be Fed* (New York, NY: William Morrow and Co., 1992).

dissemination of true knowledge about nutrition. But it is a small step in the right direction.

FOOD GUIDE PYRAMID
A GUIDE TO DAILY FOOD CHOICES

US DEPARTMENT OF AGRICULTURE
(ISSUED APRIL 28, 1992)

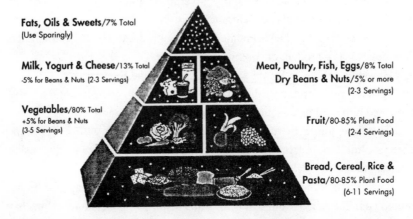

Fats, Oils & Sweets/7% Total
(Use Sparingly)

Milk, Yogurt & Cheese/13% Total
-5% for Beans & Nuts (2-3 Servings)

Vegetables/80% Total
+5% for Beans & Nuts
(3-5 Servings)

Meat, Poultry, Fish, Eggs/8% Total
Dry Beans & Nuts/5% or more
(2-3 Servings)

Fruit/80-85% Plant Food
(2-4 Servings)

**Bread, Cereal, Rice &
Pasta**/80-85% Plant Food
(6-11 Servings)

In addition to the books and guides outlined above, two LDS authors—Marc Sorenson, Ph.D. and Earl Updike—have recently written substantive and popular books about plant-centered diets.[1] Their messages are like those mentioned above—a healthy diet consists of plant food that is high in fiber, low in fat and low in protein.

---

[1] Sorenson, M., *Mega Health* (Ivans, UT: National Institutes of Fitness, 1992); Updike, E., *The Mormon Diet, A Word of Wisdom* (Springville, UT: Cedar Fort, Inc., 1991); The Mormon Diet Cookbook (Springville, UT: Cedar Fort, Inc., 1992).

THE NEW FOUR FOOD GROUPS
BY THE PHYSICIANS COMMITTEE FOR
RESPONSIBLE MEDICINE

Because of the misinformation and distortions that confuse the American public about a healthy food plan, an organization called the Physicians Committee for Responsible Medicine announced in a Washington, DC press conference on April 16, 1991 a sound food plan that incorporates the new scientific information on nutrition.[1]

The Physicians Committee for Responsible Medicine consists of 3,400 physicians and 60,000 lay members who have no vested interest in the promotion of lifestyle changes. They feel, as I do, that this diet change needs to be presented to and promoted in every household in America.

Led by Dr. Neal Barnard, the press conference in Washington DC included nutritional scientists and researchers who had made notable advances in the past decade. Among those present were Dr. Denis Burkitt, known for the discovery of a type of lymphoma found in children and who first established the link between certain cancers and a fiber-deficient diet.

Dr. T. Colin Campbell, professor of Nutritional Sciences at Cornell University and co-director of the China-Oxford-Cornell Project on Nutrition, Health and the Environment (also know as the China Health Project) was also present. His massive China study is a major report that documents that cancer, diabetes, stroke, hypertension and heart disease risks are much lower in people who eat food containing 10-15 per cent fat and little or no cholesterol.

Dr. Oliver Alabaster, Director of the Institute of Disease Prevention at George Washington University and author of *The Power of Prevention* was also present to promote this food guide.

At the press conference, it was pointed out that the old guideline with the "Basic Four Food Groups" of meat, dairy products, fruits and vegetables was out-dated and contrary to the best possible health. Disease, premature death

---

[1] Physicians Committee for Responsible Medicine, *New Four Food Groups*, PO Box 6322, Washington, DC, 20015.

and obesity were the result of this old guideline which had been promoted for almost forty years. It needed to be replaced by a better guideline which had been recently developed by the Physicians Committee and which they called the "New Four Food Groups." These are described below.

1. WHOLE GRAINS
(5 or more servings a day)

This group includes bread, rice, pasta, hot or cold cereal, corn, millet, barley, bulgur, buckwheat groats, and tortillas. Build each of your meals around a hearty grain dish—grains are rich in fiber and other complex carbohydrates, as well as proteins, B vitamins and zinc. Serving/size examples: 1/2 cup hot cereal or 1 ounce dry cereal or 1 slice bread.

2. LEGUMES
(2 to 3 servings a day)

Legumes—which is another name for beans, peas, and lentils—are all good sources of fiber, protein, iron, calcium, zinc, and B vitamins. This group also includes chickpeas, baked and refried beans, soy milk, tofu, tempeh, and texturized vegetable protein. Serving/size examples: 1/2 cup cooked beans or 4 ounces tofu or tempeh or 8 ounces soy milk.

3. VEGETABLES
(3 or more servings a day)

Vegetables are packed with nutrients: They provide vitamin C, beta-carotene, riboflavin, iron, calcium, fiber, and other vitamins. Dark green, leafy vegetables such as broccoli, collards, kale, mustard and turnip greens, chicory, or bok choy are especially good sources of these important nutrients. Dark yellow and orange vegetables such as carrots, winter squash, sweet potatoes and pumpkin provide extra beta-carotene. Include generous portions of a variety of vegetables in your diet. Serving/size examples: 1 cup raw vegetables or 1/2 cup cooked vegetables.

4. FRUITS

(3 or more servings a day)

Fruits are rich in fiber, vitamin C, and beta-carotene. Be sure to include at least one serving each day of fruits that are high in vitamin C—citrus fruits, melons, and strawberries are all good choices. Choose whole fruit over fruit juices, which do not contain very much fiber. Serving/size examples: 1 medium piece of fruit or 1/2 cup cooked fruit or 1/2 cup juice.

(Be sure to include a good source of vitamin B-12, such as fortified cereals or vitamin supplements.)

Taken together, these four groups provide a healthy diet approved by nutritional experts; you will notice there is no mention of meat or dairy products, for they have lost their status as being essential. Rather they are considered only optional because of the new evidence presented earlier in this book. When you follow a food plan based on grain, legumes, vegetables and fruits you will have better health and less disease. Your weight will be under control, you will look and feel better. This new food plan does not ban meat and dairy products but considers them as unnecessary and harmful in excess. It is a disease "prevention" program and it is remarkably similar to the food plan in the Word of Wisdom.

In fact, it is the same program!

WORD OF WISDOM FOOD PLAN

Readers who are members of the LDS Church need to bring together the new knowledge of nutrition and the written word in the scriptures. Only then can we help to blunt the consequences of "evils and designs which do and will exist in the hearts of conspiring men in the last days." (D&C 89:4)

By reviewing the scientific/nutritional facts presented in the recommended books outlined in Appendix C of this book, one can obtain a clear picture of the wisdom of the words in the 89th Section of the *Doctrine and Covenants* about "food." Until the last fifteen years, nutritional information was almost hidden, and even today one has to wade through much misinformation to find the truth. I applaud Dr. Cowley for his insightful magazine article of 1969.[1] Nathan Pritikin and his pioneering 1979 book should be particularly remembered. He died without realizing its impact.

The buzz words of "high-fiber," "low-fat" and "low-cholesterol" are heard everywhere: We know now that the food plan for optimum health and the prevention of premature death should derive about 10 percent of its calories from fat, about 10 percent from protein and 80 percent from complex carbohydrates. These calories are best supplied by grains, rice, potatoes, legumes, fruits and vegetables. Few or no calories should come from flesh (products of meat, eggs and milk).

The diets described in this chapter are very similar. The PCRM's New Four Food Groups, recently endorsed by our nation's best nutritional experts, follow the tenets of the Word of Wisdom. They establish a safe, sound, healthy diet, which should be implemented in every home.

Most people know that food has a great deal to with health. Many people are eager to improve their own health, but are confused because of poor and vague advice. Hopefully this book provides some answers for you.

---

[1] Cowley, R., "An 1833 Guide for the Prevention of Heart Disease," *Improvement Era*, (August 1969). (Reproduced by permission of author as Appendix A.)

CHOOSE HEALTH

WHOLE GRAINS
(5 or more servings/day)

This group includes bread, rice, pasta, hot or cold cereal, corn. millet, barley, bulgar, buckwheat groats, and tortillas. Build each of your meals around a hearty grain dish. Grains are rich in fiber and other complex carbohydrates, as well as protein, B vitamins and zinc.
Serving size: 1/2 cup hot cereal (1 ounce dry cereal, 1 slice bread).

FRUITS
(3 or more servings/day)

Fruits are rich in fiber, vitamin C, and beta-carotene. Be sure to include at least one serving each day of fruits that are high in vitamin C—citrus fruits, melons, and strawberries are all good choices. Choose whole fruits over fruit juices, which contain very little fiber.
Serving size: 1 medium piece of fruit (1/2 cup cooked fruit, 1/2 cup juice).

NEW FOUR FOOD GROUPS

LEGUMES
(2-3 servings/day)

Legumes—another name for beans, peas, and lentils—are all good sources of fiber, protein, iron, calcium, zinc, and B vitamins. This group also includes chickpeas, baked and refried beans, soy milk, tempeh, and textured vegetable protein.
Serving size: 1/2 cup cooked beans (4 ounces tofu or tempeh, 8 ounces soy milk).

VEGETABLES
(3 or more servings/day)

High in fiber, vitamin C, beta-carotene, riboflavin, iron, calcium, and other vitamins. Dark green, leafy, such as broccoli, collards, kale, mustard and turnip greens, chicory, or bok choy are especially good. Dark yellow and orange vegetables such as carrots, winter squash, sweet potatoes and pumpkins provide extra beta-carotene. Include generous portions of a variety of vegetables in your diet. *Serving size: 1 cup raw vegtbls (1/2 cup cooked vegetables).*

Be sure to include a good source of Vitamin B-12 such as fortified cereals or vitamin supplements.

PHYSICIANS COMMITTE FOR RESPONSIBLE MEDICINE
P. O. BOX 6322 • WASHINGTON, DC • 202/686-2210

CHAPTER FOURTEEN

MAKING IT ALL WORK

A drastic change in lifestyle is difficult for everyone. The very word "diet" has a bad reputation because, for the most part, it means "restriction"— a system of *no-no's* that usually ends up in failure. Most of us have tried to "diet" and have failed.

We have all tried various ploys, such as eating from a small plate, refusing second helpings, drinking water before a meal, putting the fork down between bites, and giving ourselves rewards for temporary success.

Some people try liquid diets. Others get their jaws wired shut. Many have their stomachs stapled or try bypass surgery to alter the way food is digested. Some have surgical "tummy tucks" to remove the fat. Some, in a hospital setting, even resort to complete fasting. Sadly, all of it fails.

In the past, diets were based on the theory that excess calories caused fatness, so we believed that the solution to fatness was restriction of calories. Now we know that fatness is actually the result of eating the wrong food. We are herbivores, not carnivores. When we adopt a plant centered food plan, we can eat wholesome foods that are good for us and that satisfy our hunger without restricting calories.

Like all gospel principles, the Word of Wisdom is a system of *yes-yes's*, not *no-no's*. The closer we come to following all of its principles, the happier and healthier we will be. We feel better; we are more attractive; we live longer; we have more energy.

With a lifestyle that includes proper diet and exercise, not only is one protected from premature death due to heart disease or cancer, but there are other definite benefits. First, there are real savings in the cost of food. Food bills may be cut in half. Eating food low in the food chain eliminates many of the problems of contamination, carcinogens, and adulterations found in foods high in the food chain.[1] There are less fears of about osteoporosis, constipation or vitamin deficiency. Most importantly, one has the peace of mind that one's healthy body is under control and is ready for any service or task required of it.

Since the word "diet" is so filled with negative connotation and so associated with failure, if your family is convinced about the need for a change in eating habits, you might call it "our food plan" or "The Smith Food Plan" or "The Chavez Food Plan," etc.

The truths in the Word of Wisdom food plan are expressed in just a few practical sentences. First, you can eat as much as you want, as long as you avoid the empty calories of sweets and eat foods low in fats. Second, you do not have to count calories. Third, you are eating food that is designed for your body; all the essentials for the best possible health are present.

These three principles should be discussed in your family. If they are understood, accepted and put into practice, your Food Plan will be successful.

Consider all the factors on your side. In addition to saving on your food bill, the foods are delicious and come in a wide variety. Natural foods are quick and easy to prepare—you save time. As more people adopt a healthy food plan, the profit-sensitive food industry will make the changes dictated by consumer demand.

Ready to put it all to work? Try these helpful and practical suggestions:

THE BASICS

Your eating plan should focus on basic foods that include grains, rice, potatoes, legumes, fruits and vegetables. They have minimal fat. Avoid vegetable oils, nuts, olives, and avocados for the present. Some recent unproven studies about mono-saturated fats contradict the advice about the use of nuts, olives and avocados, but for the present I would urge you to avoid them.

---

[1] Duggan R., "Dietary Intake of Pesticides in the United States," *Pesticides Monitoring Journal*, 2:140-152, (1969); Regenstein, L., *How to Survive in America, the Poisoned* (Acropolis Books, 1982); Carson, W., "New Dangers in Mother's Milk," *Time* (April 7, 1986).

STARTING OUT RIGHT

Make breakfast your main meal so you can start the day with energy. Try whole-grain cereals—such as cooked oatmeal, oat bran, cooked cracked wheat, or a combination—flavored with raisins and skim milk. That kind of breakfast replenishes the glycogen in your body cells, boosting your energy for a long morning of activity. It's worth getting up a few minutes earlier to make breakfast a major meal!

A MIDDAY BREAK

Lunch can pose some challenges. If your children are in school, look into the school lunch program, and encourage your school to implement the Food Guide Pyramid program recently developed by the U.S. Department of Agriculture. It's easier to arrange a healthy lunch if your children can take lunches from home.

Need some ideas? Try tomato burgers on whole wheat bread, or bean sandwiches prepared in a variety of ways. When the weather is cold, provide a thermos of hot vegetable soup and a heated bagel, cooked brown rice, or a baked potato. Lunch should always include a variety of raw vegetables, served plain or as a salad. Cauliflower, broccoli, cabbage, carrots, celery, onions, tomatoes, turnips, and even raw potatoes are all delicious.

FOR SUPPER (DINNER)

Get a good cookbook. You'll be successful if you plan your evening meal with the help of a good cookbook that mirrors what you and your family like in a plant-centered food plan; there are a number of such cookbooks on the market.

For best results, let your family get involved! Ask for their suggestions, and let them help plan meals and shop for food. Use a variety of grains, rice, legumes, breads, fruits, and vegetables. Potatoes, brown rice, sweet potatoes, beans, corn, and various whole grains can be cooked in advance and stored in the refrigerator for a quick dinner.

PLAN FOR GREAT SNACKS

The whole family should be free to eat whatever is in the house—so get rid of high-fat cookies, snack crackers, chips, cheese, and dips. Replace those high-cholesterol offerings with low-fat crackers, pretzels, air-popped popcorn (without butter) and fresh and dried fruits for snacks. Replace peanut butter with apple butter. Use skim milk or, if your children are older, try diluted skim soy milk; buy "lite" soy milk (1 percent or 2 percent), then add one to two parts water to every part of soy milk. You'll find that diluted skim soy milk is a little sweeter than cow's milk, contains no cholesterol, and does not cause allergic reactions.

TAKE ANOTHER LOOK AT EGGS

The white portion of an egg is free from fat and cholesterol and is acceptable as food. Throw away the yolks, or feed them to your cat or dog, who can eat them without harm. If a recipe calls for eggs, double the number and use only the whites. You might also try cooking with "Ener-G," an economical egg replacement available in health food stores and some supermarkets.

Read the labels of processed foods found in grocery stores. If the calories in the food represent more than 20 percent fat, don't buy it; 10 percent is an even better limit. If you're confused, use the formula given earlier in this book to calculate fat percentages. Be sure that your fat calculation does not represent a percentage of fat based on weight; it should be based on percentage of calories.

Whatever you do, don't rely on labels that represent food as "reduced fat" or "lite"; remember that there is plenty of misinformation disseminated by the food industry.

Establish regular meal times to help regulate your family's food needs. Small children have relatively high energy needs and small stomachs, so plan for healthy between-meal snacks for them. As long as you plan ahead at home and monitor what happens at school, you should be able to keep things under control.

Avoid mind games. Don't use food as a reward or as a pacifier. Most important, be an example and eat, at home and away from home, the food that's healthy. Instead of criticizing or nagging your family members, offer plenty of love and support. Help make a healthy food plan a pleasant, positive experience for everyone.

GET MOVING!

Plan for moderate but regular exercise. One of the best exercises you can do is walking. You can also use an indoor stationary bicycle when the weather is bad. Remember, though, that exercise alone is not enough. In *Running Without Fear*, Dr. Kenneth Cooper pointed out that famous runner and author Jim Fixx died suddenly of a heart attack while running. He had always been a tremendous exerciser, but had not followed a plant-centered food plan. His cholesterol was 254. An autopsy revealed that he had severe coronary atherosclerosis, with one coronary artery 90 percent closed. We can take an important lesson from his untimely death: "both" exercise and proper eating are important for good health.

LAST BUT NOT LEAST

Let's take the lead in educating expectant mothers about proper food plans during pregnancy, as well as healthy foods they can feed their infants and children. Let's supervise and instruct our children, blessing them with the knowledge that can give them long lives of productive service.

Above all, remember that your physical body is largely what you eat. While we still have a lot to learn, the essentials of a sensible plant-centered food plan have been outlined in the scriptures, have been documented by past and present LDS Church leaders, and have been confirmed by overwhelming medical and scientific evidence.

CONCLUSION: MY HEART

The truths I present in this book have come to me not merely through professional training and practice, but also through personal experience. As I reflect on these truths, I remember a crushing chest pain. It was excruciating, and I knew that I was having a heart attack. I had seen its effects on hundreds of my patients, but this time it was happening to me. I'd had a quadruple bypass just seven years earlier, but now I was in trouble again. My son sped me to a local hospital and, after emergency treatment, I was evacuated by helicopter to the large Phoenix hospital where I had my original surgery.

I underwent emergency angiography, during which time a small tube was again threaded through an artery in my groin to my heart; it was uncomfortable, and I was anxious. It revealed that my left coronary artery was 90 percent blocked. The cardiologist attempted to open the artery with balloon angioplasty, but was unsuccessful.

Therefore, I underwent a second open-heart surgery; the surgeons performed two more bypasses, using the last available vein in my leg and an artery from my chest wall. Having heart surgery a second time made the operation technically more difficult, and it took me longer to recover. But I survived. Two weeks later when I looked in the mirror for the first time after the heart attack, I was jolted by what I saw. I didn't look like myself. I didn't even look like my father. I looked like my grandfather.

What had gone wrong? I was only fifty-nine years old at the time of my first heart surgery. I had always been a faithful exerciser; I gave my cardiovascular system a workout at least four times a week, bringing my heart to 80 percent of its maximum capacity by jogging or playing tennis—just like the experts suggested.

I didn't know it then, but now I know what went wrong. I ate the wrong foods. It takes more than regular exercise to maintain a healthy heart. It also requires a plant-centered diet, a food plan like the one proclaimed 160 years ago in the Word of Wisdom.

Following my first heart surgery, I started a plant-centered diet twice. I failed, because I loaded up on too many raw fruits and vegetables—something that will upset the hardiest of stomachs. After my second heart surgery, I centered my diet on grains, the "staff of life," and added to my diet cooked rice, potatoes, whole wheat bread, beans and cereals, supplemented by well-tolerated cooked and raw fruits and vegetables. In essence, I learned to follow the food plan available to all of us in the Word of Wisdom.

AS A PHYSICIAN, I HAVE LEARNED THAT THE HUMAN BODY IS A MARVELOUS AND RUGGED BIOLOGIC MACHINE, ESPECIALLY WHEN IT IS CARED FOR AND TREATED PROPERLY. I ALSO UNDERSTAND AND APPRECIATE THAT THE BODY WILL, WITH NEGLECT AND ABUSE, BECOME PREMATURELY WORN OUT, CAUSING MISERY, SUFFERING AND EVEN DEATH. BY PERSONAL EXPERIENCE AND SUBSEQUENT RECENT SCIENTIFIC DOCUMENTATION, I KNOW THAT A HEALTHY HEART REQUIRES BOTH A PROPER DIET AND EXERCISE. THE EVIDENCE IS OVERWHELMING.

As a young doctor, I was assigned to perform autopsies at hospitals in the Minneapolis area. One of the things that impresses me even now was the frequent presence of atherosclerosis in the blood vessels.

Since those days more than forty years ago, there has been a veritable explosion of medical knowledge about the cause and prevention of heart disease and cancer. What we have learned through decades of the most sophisticated scientific and medical research is the same information that was given to a young prophet 160 years ago.

APPENDIX A

AN 1833 GUIDE FOR THE PREVENTION OF HEART DISEASE

by Ray Cowley, M.D.[1]

The blood of man, which delivers oxygen and nutrition to billions of body cells, requires an unfailing propulsion source to drive it through the many miles of blood channels on its never-ceasing circulatory route. This driving force, the human heart, is a complex dual circuit pump with unidirectional valves that is responsive on an instant's notice to every body need.

In addition to this rapidly responsive capability, durability of an unbelievable degree is required for the span of a lifetime. Yet the healthy heart has these qualities in surplus amounts. The pump action is provided by muscles that contract forcefully and rhythmically under the influence of self-generated electrical impulses. Provide these heart muscles with sufficient oxygen and proper nutrients via a good blood supply, and, in the absence of chance disease or injury, they will outlast [an] average life span today.

The blood flow to heart muscles is through coronary arteries originating directly from the large aorta. These are the first arteries supplied by freshly oxygenated and nutritionally renewed blood. If the heart's blood supply is diminished slightly, it cannot respond maximally to stress. If it is diminished more, severe disability and painful angina pectoris or failure may ensue.

If it is cut off completely, the heart muscles in the deprived area will die; and if the whole person survives, they are replaced by functionless scar tissue.

---

[1]Cowley, Ray, M.D., "An 1833 Guide for the Prevention of Heart Disease," *Improvement Era* (August 1969), pp. 60-63.

An abrupt closure of a coronary artery produces death in approximately thirty percent of those so afflicted before they can reach a hospital. Thirty to forty percent of those reaching a hospital alive will subsequently succumb, with an overall mortality rate of approximately fifty percent. This abrupt cessation of blood supply to a portion of the heart muscle is called a heart attack (coronary occlusion or myocardial infarction). Almost all cases of this nature are caused by hardening (atherosclerosis) of the coronary arteries, which results in a clot or atherosclerotic plaque plugging the vessel. This condition is such a frequent occurrence that it is the leading cause of death in the United States, with half a million Americans dying annually from its onslaught.

Atherosclerosis, or hardening of the arteries, occurs in many areas of the body, but it is in the vital areas of the body that in many cases the disastrous effects of this disease are first manifest (heart-coronary occlusion and brain-stroke). Atherosclerosis is an abnormal deposition of fatty substances in the normally smooth, strong inner wall of arteries, with fat (lipids), protein, and cholesterol being the chief chemicals present. The very high death rate for those with this disease continues unchecked despite maximum research effort and much money expended to improve the treatment results. This process can be prevented, however, and the emphasis should logically be in this direction.

The process of atherosclerosis was once thought to be an inevitable and irreversible result of aging, but it is neither of these, and the facts regarding this have only recently been established.

This type of heart disease is primarily seen in males, with increasing numbers of cases being seen in younger age groups (30's, 40's and 50's) during the past two decades. Although females are apparently protected from heart attack before menopause by special hormones, afterward they become as vulnerable as the male, with an even higher mortality rate.

The story of the search for the cause of this medical problem is a fascinating one, and many answers are now known. Highlighting the facts is this report from *The Mayo Clinic Proceeding*:

> I would like now to dispose of two ideas that have fairly wide acceptance among physicians. One is that atherosclerosis is an invariable accompaniment of the aging vascular system. The other is that the disease is irreversible.

Neither is true. Observations in man as well as experimental animals over many years have shown that atherosclerosis can be fact be reversed. The mechanism by which such reversal can be effected have been largely of a *dietary nature.* Our views on atherosclerosis based on a painstaking, sometimes halting, and often confusing marshalling of data leave no room for doubt that this disease need not be a necessary part of the aging vascular system. Atherosclerosis is preventable and reversible. (Vol. 40, November 1965, p. 815)

Why is this epidemic of heart disease occurring in the United States and not at all or to a lesser degree in other countries of the world? The United States has become a dangerous country to live in from this standpoint. A recent worldwide survey of mortality statistics revealed that the U.S. mortality rate was exceeded by only one other country. The entire reason for this high mortality rate was coronary heart disease. One might assume that discovery of control measures for so widespread a disease would be simple, but the uninspired mind of man most often learns truth through the pathway of trial and error, and this is a tedious, costly, and difficult process.

The gathering of scientific data began in a very preliminary manner in 1908 when a Russian scientist, Ignatovski, noted a much higher incidence of coronary atherosclerosis among the wealthy class in Russia than was found in the peasant population. He studied this situation thoroughly and reported that the high incidence of heart disease among the rich was related to a high dietary intake of meat and butterfat. He was wise before the times would allow and was silenced by disbelieving colleagues who could not accept his finding that the "best foods" in the diet were responsible for such a devastating disease process. This original and correct thought was subdued by the forces of ignorance, and for three decades little work was done along this line until the pressing urgency of the burgeoning number of cases in the USA demanded attention.

An American medical missionary working in China in the 1930's and 40's was struck by the lack of this disease there as compared to the United States and again sought the answer. His conclusion was that dietary differences played the primary role, with too much saturated fat in the American diet possibly being the major cause. (Saturated fats are usually solid at room temperature and originate primarily in animals and fowls. The lean meat is surrounded and penetrated by this fat, and complete separation of lean and fat in the kitchen is literally impossible.)

The World Health Organization (WHO) then conducted a multi-country survey of this problem spanning 10 years of time. The survey included such countries as Italy and Japan, where the incidence of this disease is twenty-fold less than in the United States. (When inhabitants of these two countries, and others, migrate to the U.S. and adopt their new country's eating habits, their heart attack rate rises within ten years.) The conclusion derived from this study was that there is a "probable" relationship between a high saturated fat intake and a high incidence of coronary atherosclerosis. (*Journal of Chronic Diseases*, Vol. 4 October 1956, p. 364.) The results of this study were widely accepted and the "probable" relationship became "definite" in the minds of many.

An enlightening sequel to the WHO study appeared two years later and demonstrates the difficulty of correctly interpreting masses of data. Two statisticians from the Rockefeller Research Institute could not accept the conclusions published by WHO, and they received permission to reanalyze their data. The results of the reevaluation were published in the *New York State Medical Journal*, Volume 59 (1958), page 2343. Whereas WHO studied 27 countries, they included only six in their final analysis. Furthermore, they utilized figures for saturated fat "available" rather than estimating the amount "ingested" (which may vary widely, depending on cooking habits). Correction for these two factors showed that death rates from coronary occlusion were more closely related to increased intake of animal protein in the diet than to saturated fat content. (Animal protein refers to the lean portion of animal meat products.)

There are now large numbers of investigations completed and published that attest to this revised conclusion. It is essential to consider too much meat as a whole, not just the fat portion, as the most important cause of coronary atherosclerosis in the U.S. Other factors do enter into the picture, such as diabetes, high blood pressure, heredity, and smoking, but diet is by far the most important one. There is now wide-spread medical agreement that proper dietary control would very significantly and rapidly reduce this serious problem.

In the journal *Nutritional Reviews* (vol. 18, November 1960) is a study of coronary heart disease in African Bantu natives compared to Englishmen living in the same area. The English males have 26 times as much coronary disease as the Bantus, and their diet is incriminated as the cause. The English ingest large amount of meat of animal origin and the Bantus eat very little meat, subsisting on grain, vegetables, and fruit for the most part.

From Finland comes further data in the *Acta Medica Scandinavica* (Vol. 139 [1961], page 364). In World War II, the population of Finland was on strict food rationing. During this time, the previously significant incidence of coronary heart disease dropped almost to zero. When the rationing stopped and meat and butterfat again again became plentiful, the incidence of coronary occlusions increased 584 percent in six years.

A most revealing (and alarming) study emerged from the Korean War. Special studies of the coronary arteries to determine the degree of atherosclerosis present were carried out in 500 American males and 500 [Korean] males killed in action. The average age of both groups was 22. Virtually none of the Koreans had coronary artery abnormalities, whereas 90 percent of the American males had atherosclerosis of their coronary arteries. In half of these Americans the atherosclerosis was severe enough to be considered medically significant. (*Journal of the American Medical Association*, Vol. 152 [1953], p. 1090.) Personal communication in 1966 with a Korean health authority disclosed that only one case of coronary occlusion had been encountered in 15 years at the largest medical center in Seoul, Korea. Contrast this to the very large numbers of patients with this disease constantly present in every general hospital in the United States. Again, the obvious reason for this wide difference is the Korean diet of vegetables, fruits, and seafood, whereas meat and butterfat are scarce in Korea. (Butterfat has been mentioned several times, and there is now sufficient evidence to conclude that this animal origin food product is one of the dietary factors producing coronary atherosclerosis.)

A study dealing with the effect of deliberate dietary alterations in humans needs to be mentioned. At the annual meeting of the American College of Physicians in Philadelphia, Pennsylvania, in 1962, a panel of prominent heart specialists presented the results of the following study.

Several hundred patients already diagnosed as having sufficient atherosclerosis to produce signs of symptoms of disease were divided into two equal groups. Those in one group continued their usual American diet, and the other group was placed on a diet containing no animal origin meat and only small amount of fowl origin meat. Seafood, grains, vegetables, and fruit were the primary foods. Those two groups were carefully observed for ten years. The group on the low meat diet showed a much lower rate of progression of their atherosclerosis, a much reduced death rate, and some participants even recovered in part or completely from the symptoms of their disease. The other group showed the expected progressive downhill course of the average American with this disease who continues to eat [the] average American diet. The panel concluded that if the epidemic of coronary atherosclerosis in the USA is to be curtailed, the American populace must begin at a young age to eat the low meat type of diet that was tested for ten years.

A recent list of 489 articles on the disease atherosclerosis, many showing the relationship of diet to the formation of atherosclerosis, is available to anyone interested in further pursuit of this subject. (*Laboratory Investigation*, Vol. 18, May 1968, pp. 629-39.) This mass of research data shows a strong relationship between a high incidence of atherosclerosis and dietary changes incident to improved economic status, such as the greater consumption of animal protein, saturated fat, refined carbohydrates, and the decreased use of cereal grains. (See pages 623 to 628 of this same journal, "Diet and Atherosclerosis.") Although this relationship is now supported by almost incontrovertible proof, the medical profession has been slow to accept findings that decimate a long-standing and traditional medical dictum that a steady and large dietary intake of animal or fowl origin meat is essential to good health.

In times or places where available foods are limited in variety, quantity, or quality, such as in rice-based cultures or famine conditions, meat of animal or fowl origin may become an important source, and indeed, a necessary protein source, if available. For affluent contemporary cultures, however, the prudent diet with protein sources of fish, seafood, whole grain (especially wheat), and non-fat milk solids is adequate in protein content, less costly, and does not carry with it the specter of early and severe atherosclerosis.

Although we cannot know with certainty all the reasons that our Father in heaven has given us clear-cut and specific instructions to eat *little or no meat of animal or fowl origin*, one fact is certain: Daily consumption of animal— and fowl—origin meat and fat may be an important cause of coronary heart disease.

"Yea, Flesh also of beasts and of the fowls of the air, I, the Lord, have ordained for the use of man with thanksgiving; nevertheless they are to be used *sparingly*;

"And it is pleasing unto me that they should not be used, *only in times of winter, or of cold, or famine.*

"All grain is ordained for the use of man and of beasts, to be the staff of life, not only for man but for the beasts of the field, and the fowls of the heaven, and all wild animals that run or creep on the earth;

"*And these hath God made for the use of man only in times of famine and excess of hunger.*" (D&C 89:12-15 Italics added*)

The Word of Wisdom is a remarkable revelation brought forth in 1833 as a health guide. It has remained completely unchanged in 136 years, with medical research repeatedly attesting to its validity. Contrast this to man-produced medical information of that same time period, of which the vast majority has been replaced or necessarily changed as research has revealed fallacies therein. The items of medical literature from that time that remain intact today are of value only as museum pieces.

Had Joseph Smith sought help in 1833 from the best medical authorities in the world, used their ideas in the preparation of such a document, and then declared it to be of divine origin, he would have been branded a fraud prior to the turn of the century. The only conceivable explanation for Section 89 of the Doctrine and Covenants is that it came from a highly advanced and infallible source of intelligence beyond this earth. The contents of this section should be carefully studied, and personal eating and living habits should be formulated on the basis of advice given therein, for this is of a certainty a divinely inspired guide to good health and long life, with transcendant rewards for compliance that should induce the most skeptical to put it to an honest test.

*Verses 13 and 15 leave no room for rationalization regarding the amount of meat that we in our warm houses, warm cars, and land of plenty should eat. (See also Sidney B. Sperry, *Doctrine and Covenants Compendium* [Bookcraft, 1960] pp. 455-56.)

POSITION OF THE AMERICAN DIETETIC ASSOCIATION: VEGETARIAN DIETS[1]
(REAFFIRMED OCTOBER 1992)

POSITION STATEMENT AND SUMMARY PAPER

It is the position of The American Dietetic Association that vegetarian diets are healthful and nutritionally adequate when appropriately planned.

The attention focused today on personal health habits is unprecedented, as more and more Americans *adopt health-promoting life-styles* that include alterations in diet and exercise patterns. Simultaneously, there has been an *increased interest in vegetarian diets*. A considerable body of scientific data suggests positive relationships between vegetarian life-styles and risk reduction for several chronic degenerative diseases, such as *obesity, coronary artery disease, hypertension, diabetes mellitus, colon cancer, and others*. The high incidence of such diseases in industrialized nations, as compared with other cultures, warrants special attention to diet and other factors in life-styles that may vary between vegetarians and nonvegetarians.

It should be recognized that both vegetarian and nonvegetarian diets have the potential to be either beneficial or detrimental to health. Sound nutrition planning may result in risk reduction and control of some diseases and conditions by dietary measures, whereas poorly planned or haphazard diets increase the likelihood of diet-related disorders of deficiency or excess. However, in addition to the possible health benefits of some vegetarian diets,

---

[1] Approved by the House of Delegates on October 18, 1987, and reaffirmed in October 1992 as the official position of the ADA. The American Dietetic Association authorizes republication of this position, in its entirety, provided full and proper credit is given.

consideration may also be given to ecological, economical, and philosophical or ethical reasons for adopting such a diet. It may be easier, as well as more acceptable, for some individuals to meet the Guidelines for Americans by following a vegetarian diet rather than a nonvegetarian diet.

Vegetarianism, generally defined as the abstinence from meat, fish, and fowl, encompasses a wide variety of eating patterns involving degrees of animal food avoidance. *Most vegetarian diets in the United States are high in fiber and low in total fat, saturated fat, and cholesterol.* The most common types of vegetarians, or vegans, who abstain from meat, fish, fowl, dairy products, and eggs, must ensure that caloric intakes are adequate to maintain desirable body weight, particularly throughout childhood. *Vegans must be certain to include an appropriate source of vitamin B-12 in their diets. In addition, if their exposure to sunshine is limited, a vitamin D supplement may be indicated.*

In planning a vegetarian diet, one should choose a wide variety of foods from the major food groups. *The foods may include fresh fruits, vegetables, whole grain breads and cereals, nuts and seeds, legumes, low-fat dairy products or fortified soy substitutes, and a limited number of eggs*, if desired. Vegetarians are advised to keep their intake of low nutrient-dense foods to a minimum. Consumption of a good food source of ascorbic acid with meals will further enhance absorption of available iron. Iron-deficiency anemia has been known to occur in both vegetarians and nonvegetarians. Mixtures of proteins from grains, vegetables, legumes, seeds, and nuts eaten over the course of the day complement one another in their amino acid profiles without the necessity of precise planning and complementation of proteins within each meal, as the recently popular "combined proteins theory" has urged.

Finally, those whose nutrient needs are especially high because of growth, lactation, or recovery from illness can generally meet their nutrient requirements on vegetarian diets containing dairy products. Those who follow vegan or vegan-like diets must take care to ensure adequate intakes of calories, vitamin B-12, and vitamin D. *Vegetarians and nonvegetarians alike whose infants are exclusively breast fed beyond 4 to 6 months of age should give the infants vitamin D and iron supplements.*

TECHNICAL SUPPORT PAPER

The attention focused today on personal health habits is unprecedented, as more and more Americans adopt health-promoting life-styles that include alterations in diet and exercise patterns. Simultaneously, there has been a marked rise in interest in vegetarian diets. *A considerable body of scientific data suggests positive relationships between vegetarian life-styles and risk reduction for several chronic degenerative diseases and conditions, such as obesity, coronary artery disease, hypertension, diabetes mellitus, colon cancer, and others.* The high incidence of such diseases in industrialized nations, as compared with other cultures, warrants special attention to diet and other factors in life-styles that may vary between vegetarians and nonvegetarians.

It is the position of The American Dietetic Association that vegetarian diets are healthful and nutritionally adequate when appropriately planned.

Both vegetarian and nonvegetarian diets have the potential to be either beneficial or detrimental to health. Sound nutrition planning may result in risk reduction and control of some diseases and conditions by dietary measures, whereas poorly planned or haphazard diets increase the likelihood of diet-related disorders of deficiency or excess. However, in addition to the possible health benefits of some vegetarian diets, consideration may also be given to ecological, economical, and philosophical or ethical reasons for adopting such a diet. It may be easier, as well as more acceptable, for some individuals to meet the Dietary Guidelines for Americans by following a vegetarian diet rather than a nonvegetarian diet.[1]

VEGETARIANISM IN PERSPECTIVE

There is no single vegetarian eating pattern. From the standpoint of nutritional health, vegetarian diets are distinguished from one another by (a) the extent to which the foods included vary, (b) the degree to which the diets

---

[1] Carlson, E., Kipps, M., Lockie, A., and Thomson. J: A, "Comparative Evaluation of Vegan, Vegetarian and Omnivore Diets," *J Plant Foods* 6:89, (1985).

are planned to correspond to the findings of nutritional sciences, and (c) the health attitudes and practices that are associated with the diets.

Vegetarian diets differ in the extent to which they avoid animal products. Veganism, or total vegetarianism, completely excludes meat, fish, fowl, eggs, and dairy products. Lactovegetarianism is the avoidance of only meat, fish, or fowl. Semi-vegetarian patterns allow limited amounts of most animal foods.

In addition to proscriptions on animal foods, some vegetarian diets also incorporate restrictions on other foods and beverages, such as honey, alcohol, caffeinated beverages, highly processed foods, and foods that are grown or processed nonorganically or with certain additives and preservatives. Finally, some patterns include the addition of special foods or practices that are thought to have unique health promotive or curative properties. Included are vitamin-mineral supplements, dietary fiber and essential fatty acid supplements, health foods, herbal teas, and practices such as periodic fasting.

Since vegetarianism is a term that encompasses such a wide variety of eating patterns, nutrition assessment of such diets is difficult without information about specific food avoidances and health-related attitudes and practices. The differences may have a significant impact on nutritional status.[1]

Studies of vegetarians indicate that this population generally has lower mortality rates from several chronic degenerative diseases than do nonvegetarians. It is likely that the effects are due not to diet alone but also to a healthy life-style, including desirable weight, regular physical activity, and abstinence from smoking, alcohol, and illicit drugs, with adequate health monitoring.[2, 3, 4, 5]

Even though the health benefits of a vegetarian diet make it attractive from a nutrition standpoint, this does not preclude the possibility of obtaining similar health benefits from a prudent nonvegetarian diet if it can be planned

[1] Dwyer, J.T., "1983 Nutrition status and alternative lifestyle diets with special reference to vegetarianism in the USA," In Reichaig, M., ed, *CRC Handbook of Nutritional Supplements*, Vol.1, Human Use (Boca Raton, FL: CRC Press, 1983), pp. 343-410.

[2] Kahn, R.H., Phillips, R.L., Snowdon, D.A., and Choi, W., "Association between reported diet and all cause mortality. Twenty-one year follow up on 27,530 adult Seventh Day Adventists," *Am J Epidermiol* 119:775, (1984).

[3] Phillips, R.L., Garfinkel, L., Kuzma, J.W., Beeson, W.L., Lotz, T., and Brin, B., "Mortality among California Seventh Day Adventists for selected cancer sites," *J Nat Cancer Inst.* 65:1097, (1980).

[4] "The diet and all causes death rate in the Seven Countries study," *Lancet* 2:58, (1981).

[5] Kromhout, D., Bosscheiter, E.B., and de Lezenne Coulander. C., "Dietary fiber and 10 year mortality from coronary heart disease, cancer, and all causes," *Lancet* 2:518, (1982).

in accordance with the Dietary Guidelines for Americans. *However, in addition to health aspects, consideration that may lead to the adoption of a vegetarian diet include: ecological implications of eating low on the food chain with regard to preservation of the environment or for the perceived solution to world hunger problems by decreasing the demand on the world's food resources; economic reasons, since diets low in animal proteins are typically less expensive than meat-based diets; and philosophical or ethical reasons, which include animal rights issues and attitudes toward violence. Still other individuals are motivated by religious beliefs.*

IMPLICATIONS FOR HEALTH PROMOTION

Mortality from coronary artery disease is lower in vegetarians than in nonvegetarians.[1, 2] Total serum cholesterol and LDL cholesterol levels are usually lower, while HDL cholesterol and triglyceride levels vary, depending on the type of vegetarian diet that is followed.[3, 4, 5, 6] Vegetarian diets that are typically very low in fat and cholesterol may decrease levels of apoproteins A, B, and E.[7] Platelet composition and possible platelet functions may vary, and plasma viscosity may be decreased.[8] Such effects may be attributed to the vegetarian's lower intake of total fat, saturated fat, and cholesterol, along with

---

[1] "Burt, M.L., and Sweetnam, P.M. Vegetarianism, dietary fiber, and mortality," *Am J Clin Nutr.*, 36:873, (1982).

[2] Phillips, R.L., Kuzma, J.W., Beeson, W.L., and Lotz, T., "Influence of selection versus lifestyle on risk of fatal cancer and cardiovascular disease among Seventh Day Adventists," *Am J Epidemiol* 112:296, (1980).

[3] Sacks, F.M., Ornish, D., Rosner, B., McLanahan, S., Castelli, W.P., and Kass, E.H., "Plasma lipoproteins in vegetarians: The effect of intake of dietary fat," *JAMA* 254:1337, (1985).

[4] Knuiman, J.T., and West, C.E., "The concentration of cholesterol in serum and in various serum lipoproteins in macrobiotic, vegetarian, and nonvegetarian men and boys," *Atherosclerosis* 43:71, (1982).

[5] Masarei, J.R.L., Rouse, I.L., Lynch, W.J., Robertson, K., Vandongen, R., and Beilin, L.J., "Effects of a lactoovovegetarian diet on serum concentrations of cholesterol, triglyceride, HDL-C, HDL-2-C, HDL-3-C, apoprotein B, and Lp(a)," *Am J Clin Nutr* 40:468, (1984).

[6] Cooper, R.S., Goldberge, R.B., Trevisan, M., Tsong, Y., Liu, K., Stamler, J., Rubenstein, A., and Scanu, A.M., "The selective lipid lowering effect of vegetarianism on low density lipoproteins in a crossover experiment," *Atherosclerosis* 44:293, (1982).

[7] Ibid.

[8] Fisher, M., Levine, P.H., Weiner, B., Ockens, I.S., Johnson, B., Johnson, M.H., Natale, A.M., Vaudreuil, C.H., and Hoogasian, J., "The effect of vegetarian diets on plasma lipid and platelet levels," *Arch inter Med* 146: 1193, (1986).

lower weight, increased physical activity, and abstinence from smoking.[1,2,3] *Vegetarians generally have lower blood pressures and lower rates of Type II diabetes than do nonvegetarians, which may decrease the risk of coronary artery disease in the vegetarian population.*

Vegetarians of the Seventh-Day Adventists faith have lower rates of mortality from colon cancer than does the general population.[4] That may be due to dietary differences which include increased fiber intake, decreased intake of total fat, cholesterol, and caffeine, increased intakes of fruits and vegetables, and, in lacto-vegetarians, increased intakes of calcium.[5] Although it is still speculative, the dietary differences, especially in vegans, may produce physiological changes that may inhibit the causal chain for colon cancer.[6,7] *Lung cancer rates are lower in many types of vegetarians because they typically do not smoke or, possibly, because of their increased intake of beta carotene or other constituents of fruits and vegetables that may also lower lung cancer risk.[8] Preliminary evidence suggests that vegetarians may be at lower risk for breast cancer, but further study is indicated.[9]*

Obesity is a complicating condition exacerbating many diseases. *Vegetarians, especially vegans, have weights that are closer to desirable*

[1] Knuiman, J.T., and West, C.E., "The concentration of cholesterol in serum and in various serum lipoproteins in macrobiotic, vegetarian, and nonvegetarian men and boys," *Atherosclerosis* 43:71, (1982).

[2] Sacks, F.M., Miller, L., Sutherland, M., Albers, J.J., Salazar, J., Foster, J.M., Samonds, K.W., and Kass, E.H., "Ingestion of egg raises plasma low density lipoproteins in free living subjects," *Lancet* 1:647, (1984).

[3] Renoud, S., Godsey, F., Dumont, E., Thevonen, C., Ortchanian, E., and Martin, J.L., "Influence on longterm diet modification on platelet function and composition on Moselle farmers," *Am J Clin Nutr* 43:136, (1986).

[4] Phillips, R.L., Garfinkel, L., Kuzma, J.W., Beeson, W.L., Lotz, T., and Brin, B., "Mortality among California Seventh Day Adventists for selected cancer sites," *J Nat Cancer Inst* 65:1097, (1980).

[5] Turjiman, N., Goodman, G.T., Jaeger, B., and Nair, P.P., "Diet nutrition intake and metabolism in populations at high and low risk for colon cancer Metabolism of bile acids," *Am J Clin Nutr* 4:937, (1984).

[6] Ibid.

[7] Adlercreutz, H., "Does fiber rich food containing animal lignan precursors protect against both colon and breast cancer? An extension of the fiber hypothesis," *Gastroenterology* 86: 761, (1984).

[8] Colditz, G.Z., Stampfer, M.J., and Willett, W.C., "Diet and lung cancer: A review of the epidemiological evidence in humans," *Arch Intern Med* 147: 157, (1987).

[9] Goldin, B.R., "The metabolism of the intestinal microflora and its relationship to dietary fat, colon and breast cancer," In Ip. C., Birt, D., Rogers, A., and Mettlin, C., eds, *Dietary Fat and Cancer* (New York, NY: Alan R. Liss, 1986).

weights than do nonvegetarians.[1] Several factors may be involved, including moderation in energy intakes, increased physical activity, and better regulation of food intake. *The high-carbohydrate, low-fat vegetarian diet, in combination with exercise, may decrease the risk of obesity.*[2]

Vegetarians are at lower risk for noninsulin-dependent diabetes, partly because they are leaner than nonvegetarians.[3, 4.] The vegetarians' high intake of complex carbohydrates, with its relatively high fiber content, improves carbohydrate metabolism, lowering basal glucose levels.[5, 6.]

Vegetarians have lower rates of hypertension than do nonvegetarians, which may be due to vegetarians' relative leanness.[7, 8.] Other aspects of life-style may also be involved,[9] such as dietary habits, increased physical activity, and abstinence from smoking.

Finally, vegetarians have lower rates of osteoporosis, kidney stones, gallstones, and diverticular disease.[10, 11, 12] Studies documenting these benefits, however, are inconclusive at this time, and reasons may be related to aspects of life-style other than diet.

[1] Bergan, J.G., and Brown, P.T., "Nutritional status of 'new' vegetarians," *J Am Diet Assoc* 76:151, (1980).

[2] Bray, G.A., "Obesity: A disease of nutrient or energy balance?" *Nutr Rev* 45:33, (1987).

[3] West, K.M., and Kalbfleisch, J.M., "Glucose tolerance, nutrition, and diabetes in Uruguay, Venezuela, Malaya, and East Pakistan," *Diabetes* 15:9, (1966).

[4] West, K.M., and Kalbdleisch, J.M. "Influence of nutritional factors on prevalence or diabetes," *Diabetes* 20:99, (1971).

[5] Stevens, J., Burgess, M.B., Kaiser, D.L., and Sheppa, C.M. "Outpatient management of diabetes mellitus with patient education to increase dietary carbohydrate and fiber," *Diabetes Care* 8:359, (1985).

[6] Munoz, J.M., "Fiber and diabetes," *Diabetes Care* 7:297, (1984).

[7] Page, L.B., "Hypertension and atherosclerosis in primitive and acculturating societies," In Hunt, J.C., ed.: *Hypertension Update* (Bloomfield, NH: Health Learning Systems, 1980).

[8] Reisin, E., Abel, R., Modan, M., Silverber, D., Eliahou, H., and Modan, B. "Effect of weight loss without salt restriction on the reduction of blood pressure in overweight hypertensive patients," *N Engl J Med* 298:1, (1978).

[9] Rouse, I.L., Beilin, L.J., Armstrong, B.K., and Vandongen, R., "Vegetarian diet, blood pressure and cardiovascular risk," *Aust NZ J Med* 14:439, (1984).

[10] Marsh, A.G., Sanchez, T.V., Mickelsen, O., Keiser, J., and Mavor G, "Cortical bone density of adult lactoovovegetarians and omnivorous women," *J Am Diet Assoc.* 76:148, (1980).

[11] Pixley, F., Wilson, D., McPerson, K., and Mann, J., "Effect of vegetarianism on development of gallstones in women," *Br Med J* 291: 11, (1985).

[12] Gear, J.S., Ware, A., Fursdon, P., Mann, J.I., Nolan, D.J., Broodribb, A.J. and Vessey, M.P., "Symptomless diverticular disease and intake of dietary fiber," *Lancet* 1: 511, (1979).

NUTRITION CONSIDERATION

The body's need for essential amino acids can be met by consumption of animal or plant sources of protein since, after absorption, amino acids from exogenous and endogenous sources combine in the body's protein pool.[1] Plant foods contain less of the essential amino acids than do equivalent quantities of animal food, but a plant-based diet provides adequate amounts of amino acids when a varied diet is consumed on a daily basis. A mixture of proteins from unrefined grains, legumes, seeds, nuts, and vegetables will complement one another in their amino acid profiles so that deficits in one are made up by another.

Intakes of different types of protein that complement one another should be eaten over the course of the day. However, since endogenous sources of amino acids are also available, it is not necessary that complementation of amino acid profiles be precise and at exactly the same meal, as the recently popular "combined proteins theory" suggested. This theory urged conscious combining of proteins at every meal with the caveat that malnutrition would ensue if this was not done within a strict time interval.[2]

Although vegetarian diets usually meet or exceed requirements for protein, they typically provide less protein than nonvegetarian diets. *This lower protein intake may be beneficial, however, and may be associated with a lower risk of osteoporosis in vegetarians* and improved kidney function in individuals with prior kidney damage.[3, 4] *Further, a lower protein intake generally translates into a lower fat diet with its inherent advantages, since foods high in protein are frequently also high in fat.*

Plant carbohydrates are accompanied by liberal amounts of dietary fiber, which has been shown to be important in the prevention and treatment of disease. Foods derived from animal sources contain no fiber. Complex carbohydrates from plants also improve glucose tolerance, as previously noted.

---

[1] Scrimshaw, N.S., "Nature or protein requirements," *J Am Diet Assoc* 54:94, (1969).

[2] Hardinge, M.G., Crooks, H., and Stare, F.I., "Nutritional studies of vegetarians: 5. Proteins and essential amino acids," *J Am Diet Assoc* 48:25, (1966).

[3] Osteoporosis Consensus Conference, National Institutes of Health, Bethesda, MD, 1984.

[4] El Nanas, A.M., and Coles, G.A., "Dietary treatment of chronic renal failure: Ten unanswered questions," *Lancet* 1:597, (1986).

Vegetarian diets that are low in animal foods are typically lower than nonvegetarian diets in total fat, saturated fat, and cholesterol, an important factor in risk reduction for heart disease and some forms of cancer. The ratio of polyunsaturated and monounsaturated fats to saturated fats is also more favorable in a largely plant-based diet.

Vegetarians and nonvegetarians alike may have difficulty meeting recommendations for iron. Absorption of dietary iron is enhanced by concurrent consumption of ascorbic acid or animal foods; it is inhibited by the intake of tea, fiber, and phytates.[1] Western vegetarians generally have better iron status than those in developing countries. The former have a relatively high intake of iron from plant foods, such as dark green leafy vegetables, iron-fortified cereals, and whole grains. They may take supplements of ascorbic acid or iron and have a greater intake of ascorbic acid from plant foods. In contrast, vegetarians in developing countries consume less ascorbic acid and animal protein, rely on low-iron food staples and consume more fiber and tea than do Westerners.[2]

The requirement for vitamin B-12 is minute, but there is no vitamin B-12 in anything that grows from the soil. It is, however, contained in all animal foods; hence, a diet that includes animal foods, such as dairy products, is unlikely to be deficient in vitamin B-12. Bacteria produce vitamin B-12 in the human gut, but it appears to be produced beyond the ileum, the site of absorption in the intestine. Ninety-five percent of what is produced is actually inactive vitamin B-12 analogs.[3] *The need for vitamin B-12 is very small, and lack of intrinsic factors is a more common cause of vitamin B-12 deficiency than lack of vitamin B-12 in the diet.*

Nevertheless, adequate vitamin B-12 intake is a legitimate concern for Western vegans. In countries where sanitary conditions are poor, contamination of foods with microbes and organisms that produce the vitamin may contribute all that is needed. In Western countries, however, where sanitary practices are better, the risk of vitamin B-12 deficiency is greater.

---

[1] International Nutritional Anemia Consultative Group, *The Effects of Cereals and Legumes on Iron Availability* (Washington, DC: Nutrition Foundation, 1982).

[2] Sanders, T.A.B., "Vegetarianism: Dietetic and medical aspects," *J Plant Foods* 5:3, (1983).

[3] Herbert, V., "Vitamin B-12; plant sources, requirements assay," In Mulch, P.B., and Johnston, P.K., Eds.; "First International Congress on Vegetarian Nutrition," *Am J Clin Nutr* 48:452, (1988).

Vegans must include a reliable source of vitamin B-12 in their diets or be at risk of eventually developing a deficiency.[1]

However, food labeling of vitamin B-12 can be misleading. The vitamin B-12 contents of most foods in the United States has been determined by use of a microbiological assay which measures not only physiologically active forms of vitamin B-12 for human subjects but also inactive vitamin B-12 analogs. By microbiological assay, as much as 80% to 94% of the so-called vitamin B-12 in fermented plant foods, such as tempeh, and in other plant foods may be inactive vitamin B-12 analogs.[2]

Some of the vitamin B-12 analogs also compete with active forms of vitamin B-12 for absorption. Thus, *vegans should supplement their diets with a source of vitamin B-12 such as a cobalamin supplement* or select appropriately fortified foods that meet the Recommended Dietary Allowances to ensure an adequate intake of the active form of the nutrient. Further research on vitamin B-12 is needed, as there is a great deal that is not understood regarding available sources of vitamin B-12 for vegans.

Calcium absorption appears to be inhibited by such plant constituents as phytic acid, oxalic acid, and fiber, but this effect may not be significant. Calcium deficiency in vegetarians is rare, and *there is little evidence to show that low intakes of calcium give rise to major health problems among the vegetarian population. One recent study has shown that vegetarians absorb and retain more calcium from foods than do nonvegetarians.*[3] *Other studies cite lower rates of osteoporosis in vegetarians than in nonvegetarians.*[4]

Reliance on sunshine alone, particularly in northern climates or in cultures where most of the body is concealed in clothing, may not provide all of the vitamin D needed to protect children against rickets.[5] For those who do not use vitamin D-fortified milk products, *a vitamin D supplement may be*

---

[1] Herbert, as just cited.

[2] Ibid.

[3] Nnakwe, N., and Kies, C., "Calcium and phosphorus utilization omnivores and lactoovovegetarians fed laboratory controlled lactoovovegetarian diets," *Nutr Rep Int* 31:1009, (1985).

[4] Marsh, A.G., Sanchez, T.V., Mickelsen, O., Keiser, J., and Mavor G., "Cortical bone density of adult lactoovovegetarians and omnivorous women," *J Am Diet Assoc* 76:148, (1980).

[5] Curtis, J.A., Kooh, S.W., Fraser, D., and Greenberg, M.L., "Nutritional rickets in vegetarian children," *Can Med Assoc J* 128:150, (1983).

necessary, especially for dark-skinned individuals and for infants whose only source of vitamin D is breast milk *after 4 to 6 months of age.*

GROUPS WITH SPECIAL NEEDS

Those whose nutrients needs are especially high because of growth, lactation, or recovery from illness will find it especially helpful to consult a registered dietitian or other qualified nutrition professional for expert help in diet planning. Infants and children who consume well-planned vegetarian diets including milk products or eggs can generally meet all of their nutritional requirements for growth. Those who follow vegan or vegan-like diets which include no animal products can be healthy, but more care must be taken to ensure adequacy. Vitamin D and iron supplements, in addition to vitamin B-12 levels sufficient to meet the Recommended Dietary Allowances, may need to be provided.[1]

Vegan diets tend to be high in bulk which makes it more challenging to meet energy needs, especially for infants, children, and adolescents.[2] Further, care must be taken to obtain enough vitamins D and B-12. A properly fortified soy product may be helpful. Both vegetarians and nonvegetarians whose infants are premature or are breast fed exclusively beyond 4 to 6 months of age should provide supplements of vitamin D and iron from birth or at least by 4 to 6 months, as medical guidance suggests. The guidelines of the American Academy of Pediatrics for supplementation of infants are helpful.[3]

Well-planned vegetarian diets are adequate for pregnant and lactating women. With both vegetarian and nonvegetarian diets, iron and folate supplements are usually necessary during pregnancy, although vegetarians frequently have greater intakes of those nutrients than do nonvegetarians.

---

[1] Vvhmeister, J.B., Register, D.D., and Sonnenberg, L.M., "Safe vegetarian diets for children," *Pediatr Clin North Am* 24:203, (1977).

[2] Truesdell, D.D., and Acosta, P.B., "Feeding the vegan infant and child," *J Am Diet Assoc* 85:837, (1985).

[3] Committee on Nutrition, American Academy of Pediatrics, "Vitamin and mineral supplement needs in normal children in the United States," *Pediatrics* 66:1015, (1980).

MEAL PLANNING

In planning vegetarian diets of any type, one should choose a wide variety of foods, which may include fruits, vegetables, whole grain food products, nuts, seeds, legumes, low-fat dairy products or fortified soy substitutes, and a limited number of eggs. Additionally, the following recommendations are made:[1,2]

- Keep the intake of low nutrient-dense foods, such as sweets and fatty foods, to a minimum.
- Choose whole or unrefined grain products whenever possible, instead of refined products.
- Use a variety of fruits and vegetables, including a good food source of vitamin C to enhance iron absorption.
- If milk products are consumed, use low-fat varieties.
- Limit intake of eggs to two to three yolks per week to ensure that cholesterol intakes are not excessive.
- For vegans, use a properly fortified food source of vitamin B-12, such as fortified soy milks or breakfast cereals, or take a cobalamin supplement.
- For infants and children, ensure adequate intakes of iron, vitamin D, and energy.
- Consult a registered dietitian or other qualified nutrition professional.

The Dietary Guidelines for Americans recommend a reduction in fat intake and an increased consumption of fruits, vegetable, and whole grains. Well-planned vegetarian diets effectively meet these guidelines and the Recommended Dietary Allowances and can be confidently embraced as a healthy dietary alternative. However, vegetarian, particularly total vegetarians, living in a nonvegetarian society such as the United States, must be aware that foods most readily available in this culture may not be those which are most appropriate for their eating patterns; thus, vegetarians must pay special attention to ensuring nutrient adequacy. Additionally, both vegetarians and nonvegetarians must obtain adequate health monitoring throughout the life cycle. *(emphasis added)*

---

[1]Committee on Nutrition, as just cited.

[2]American Dietetic Association, "Position paper on the vegetarian approach to eating," *J Am Diet Assoc* 77:61, (1980).

APPENDIX C

RECOMMENDED READING AUTHORS AND BOOKS

Some of these books are discussed in greater detail in Chapter Thirteen.

All of the authors and their books listed below are in remarkable agreement in presenting their theme:

THAT OUR AMERICAN DIET WITH ITS HIGH CONTENT OF ANIMAL PRODUCTS AND ITS SPARSENESS OF PLANT FOODS CAUSES OBESITY, ILLNESS AND PREMATURE DEATH.

TO REVERSE THIS SITUATION, WE MUST EAT A HEALTHY PLANT-CENTERED DIET, which is the food plan revealed 160 years ago as part of the Word of Wisdom.

JOHN MCDOUGALL, M.D.

The McDougall Plan. New Century Publishers, 1983. *McDougall's Medicine: A Challenging Second Opinion*. New Century Publishers, 1985. *The McDougall Program*. NAL Books, 1990.

A skeptic about nutritional facts should read Dr. McDougall's 1985 book. It is written in lucid, everyday language with documentation from recent medical literature. The other books also include good recipes.

MICHAEL KLAPER, M.D.

Pregnancy, Children and the Vegan Diet. Gentle World, Inc., Umatilla, Florida, 1987.

Anyone who is concerned about the safety of a plant-centered diet for expectant mothers and children should read this short book.

DEAN ORNISH, M.D.

Dr. Dean Ornish's Program for Reversing Heart Disease. Random House, 1990.

Anyone who has a heredity history of heart disease should read this book. It might well save your life. It has a recipe section which will attract the gourmet cook.

JOHN ROBBINS

Diet for A New America. Stillpoint Publishers, 1987. *May All Be Fed, Diet For A New World.* William Morrow & Company, 1992.

These are "must read" books. They will change your outlook on life. They did mine. I call them "wake up" books. Most of us need a little waking up.

NEAL BERNARD, M.D.

The Power Of Your Plate. Book Publishing Co., 1990.

Seventeen physicians, all nutritional experts, document the need for us to change our diets. It is short and concise.

EARL UPDIKE

The Mormon Diet, A Word of Wisdom, Cedar Fort Inc., Springville, UT, 1991. *The Mormon Diet Cookbook.* Cedar Fort Inc., Springville, Utah, 1992.

These are the first books written in forty years about the diet portion of the Word of Wisdom. The first book brings into focus the need for a proper diet. The second book shows you how to prepare proper food and enjoy it.

MARC SORENSON, ED.D.

Mega Health. National Institute of Fitness, Ivins, UT, 1992.

This is a most comprehensive book and provides valuable information about the new facts in nutrition. It also helps you implement a plant-centered diet.

OLIVER ALABASTER, M.D.

The Power of Prevention. Seville Books, Washington, D.C., 1988.

Dr. Alabaster is the Director of Disease Prevention at Georgetown University, Washington D.C. and his book gives authoritative information that reinforces the truths of plant-centered nutrition.

DENNIS REMINGTON, M.D., GARTH FISHER, PH.D., EDWARD PARENT, PH.D.

How to Lower Your Fat Thermostat. Vitality House International, 1983.

This weight control guide establishes important principles for a disease prevention program.

RAYMOND KURZWEIL

The 10% Solution for a Healthy Life. Crown Publishers, 1993.

This author describes his dilemma of heredity heart disease and maturity diabetes. He embarked on a 10% fat diet and demonstrated to his skeptical Harvard Medical School physician a remarkable turnabout. (This physician now convinced, wrote the foreword to his patient's book.) It is well researched and is another voice sending the same message—eat a plant-centered diet for disease prevention.

INDEX

Cancer xiii, xiv, 31-32, 38, 44, 49-50, 52-
56, 58-59, 80, 82, 87, 89, 93, 101, 107,
114, 131
Cannon, George Q. 12-13
Carbohydrates 24, 27, 37, 39, 120, 130
Carboloading 35, 40, 83
Carcinogens 44, 49, 54, 107
Carnivores 37, 107
Carotenoids 31
Carrots 32, 103, 109
Carthage, Illinois 9
Cattle xvi, 23, 36
Celery 32, 109
Cellulose 43
Cereal 23, 27, 35, 42, 102-3, 109, 114,
120, 124, 131, 134
Cheese 38, 49, 58, 76, 110
Chicken 43
Childbirth 6
Childbirth fever 6
Children xvi, 2, 11, 14, 19, 22, 27, 32-34,
36, 42, 47, 57-59, 64, 67, 71, 92, 94,
99, 101, 109-12, 132-35
China 38, 101, 117
Chinese 38, 71, 73
Chips 110
Chocolate 39, 55
Cholecalciferol 44
Cholesterol xi, 12, 23, 26, 29-30, 36, 39,
42-44, 46, 54, 62, 67, 69, 88, 93, 95,
97, 101, 104, 110-12, 116, 124, 127-
28, 131, 134
Church News 30, 84
Civil War 2
Cocaine 6, 22
Coffee xiv, 23-24, 34, 71
Colon 38, 43, 49, 54, 93
Colon cancer 44, 54, 123, 125, 128
Complex carbohydrates xi, 37, 40, 83,
95, 102, 104, 129-30
Constipation 43, 108

Cookbook 110, 136
Cookies 39, 110
Cool-downs 82
Cornell University 38, 101
Coronary artery disease 119, 123, 125,
127-28
Coronary artery thrombosis 62
Coumarins 31
Cow's milk 34, 38, 41, 110
Cowley, Dr. Ray G. 61, 104, 115
Crackers 110
Crank 28

D

Dairy products 43, 57, 95, 101, 103, 124,
126, 131, 134
Death rate 23-25, 53-54, 75, 80, 116,
118, 120
Degenerative disease 30, 31, 78, 86, 123,
125-26
DeMille, Cecil B. 25
Denmark 23-24
DHEA (dehydroepiandosterone) 31
Diabetes xiii, 38, 62-63, 73-78, 88, 93,
101, 118, 123, 125, 128-29, 137
Diet xiii, xiv, 11-12, 19, 23-24, 28, 30,
32, 35-36, 38-40, 42, 44, 49-55, 57-59,
61-62, 69-71, 74, 76-79, 82, 84, 88,
91-95, 97-98, 100-1, 103-4, 107-8,
114, 117-20, 123-27, 129-31, 133-37
Dips 110
Disease xiii
Disease Prevention xiii, 39, 55, 64, 92-
93, 101, 137
Diverticular disease 93, 129
Diverticulitis 43
Doctor's approval 82
Domestic Medicine 3-4
Durning, Alan 36

Research xiv, 23, 27, 30-32, 36, 44-45,
47, 50-51, 55-56, 80, 87, 94, 114, 116,
118, 120-21, 132
Retinal vascular disease 77
Riboflavin 44, 102
Rice 35, 44, 47, 58, 71, 94-95, 102, 108-
10, 114, 120
Richards, Willard 11
Robbins, John 24, 36, 58, 99, 136
Roman Empire 40

S

Salt 28, 46, 63, 88
Saturated fat xi, 61, 88, 117-18, 120, 124,
127, 131
School lunch 57-58, 109
Scott, Dave 83
Second Advent 1
Seeds 76, 94, 124, 130, 134
Seventh Day Adventists 1
Skim milk 43, 58, 95-97, 109-10
Skin blistering 6
Smith, Alvin 2
Smith, George Albert 25, 29
Smith, Hyrum 9, 10, 17
Smith, Joseph (Jr.) xiv, xv, 1, 2, 4, 11,
84, 121
Smith, Joseph F. 17-18, 20
Smith, Joseph Fielding 20, 33
Smokers 86
Smoking 49, 50, 55, 58, 70, 74, 118, 126,
128-129
Snacks 110-11
Snow, Eliza R. 14
Snow, Lorenzo 14-15, 17
Socrates 19
Sodium 30, 88
Soft drink 57, 70
Soldiers 17, 29
Soy milk 102, 110, 134

Staff of life xvi, xvii, 35, 114, 121
Stamler, Dr. Jeremiah 43
Stationary exercise bicycles 82, 84
Still, James 4
Strenuous exercise 82
Stress 25, 45, 63-64, 66, 115
Stress-treadmill 65, 80
Stretching exercise 82
Stroke xiii, xiv, 25, 38, 46, 59, 73, 76,
101, 116
Sugar 28, 30, 88
Supper 110
Surgeon General xiv, 2, 30, 87, 91
Sweets 59, 108, 134
Swimming 35, 80, 82-83

T

Tea xiv, 23-24, 34, 131
Tennis 80, 113
Thallium Stress Test 66
Thiamin 44
Thomson, Samuel 4, 5
Thymosin 31
Tobacco xiv, xvi, 23-24, 30, 34, 58, 87
Triathlete 83
Tuberculosis 2, 11
Typhoid 2

U

U.S. Department of Agriculture 31, 58,
87, 88-89, 99, 109
U.S. Department of Health and Human
Services 87-88
U.S. surplus commodities 76
United States xiv, 5, 17, 18, 20, 30, 38,
55, 57, 92, 116-19, 124, 132, 134
University of Utah 50
Uterus 38